Intercultural Readiness

Four Competences for
Working across Cultures

Intercultural Readiness

Ursula Brinkmann
Oscar van Weerdenburg

palgrave
macmillan

First published 2014 by
PALGRAVE MACMILLAN

Palgrave Macmillan in the UK is an imprint of Macmillan Publishers Limited, registered in England, company number 785998, of Houndmills, Basingstoke, Hampshire RG21 6XS.

Palgrave Macmillan in the US is a division of St Martin's Press LLC, 175 Fifth Avenue, New York, NY 10010.

Palgrave Macmillan is the global academic imprint of the above companies and has companies and representatives throughout the world.

Palgrave® and Macmillan® are registered trademarks in the United States, the United Kingdom, Europe and other countries.

ISBN 978–1–137–34697–1

This book is printed on paper suitable for recycling and made from fully managed and sustained forest sources. Logging, pulping and manufacturing processes are expected to conform to the environmental regulations of the country of origin.

A catalogue record for this book is available from the British Library.

A catalog record for this book is available from the Library of Congress.

Typeset by MPS Limited, Chennai, India.

Contents

List of Figures and Tables

Figures

Tables

Acknowledgements

This book is based on years of research and consulting in the field of intercultural management development. Many people have contributed, either by their own work on the subject and related topics, or by the direct support they provided throughout those years. Here we want to name only those who supported us directly.

We especially thank those who agreed to be interviewed and to contribute to this book with their stories and experience: Jack Barocas, Dominique Fournier, Vinciane Klein, Anneke Luijkenaar, Pieter de Man, Ann Means, Heiko Meyer and Ralf Schneider. They have shared with us numerous examples of where intercultural readiness was needed in a globalizing world, and where they demonstrated this quality as long-term expatriates and intercultural researchers, as leaders of culturally diverse teams and of internationally-operating organizations.

Throughout the development of our Intercultural Readiness Check questionnaire, we have been fortunate to work with seasoned intercultural professionals who have contributed to our work on intercultural competence development. For their insights and valuable feedback on the development of the IRC, we are especially grateful to Lisa Newson, Yvonne van der Pol and Juanita Wijnands. For their new perspectives and positive criticism we are grateful to Sundae Schneider-Bean and Tao Yue. Maarten Asser has been especially helpful in showing new ways of making the IRC valuable to different client groups, and Sjaak Pappe has helped us greatly in reflecting on how international students can benefit from feedback on their intercultural competences.

From the start of developing the IRC, we have been privileged to work with outstanding professionals from business economics and psychology. In particular, we would like to thank Karen van der Zee for her help with developing the first version of the IRC, and to Koen Beirens, Frank Brück, Johnny Fontaine, Dianne van Hemert and Wouter Schoonman for their support with developing its second version. We benefitted greatly from the fruitful discussions with Stephanie Gruttauer, Andrea Lachnik, Elisabeth Prechtl, Carsten Schermuly and Sundae Schneider-Bean about intercultural competences needed in teams. Special thanks go to Cris Rabaglia for her concise and powerful analyses of the entire IRC database.

We would like to thank Eric Vos, of Vos Text and Hypertext, for his relentless support in developing a robust and transparent online system. In writing this book, we have very much appreciated Lucille Redmond's invaluable comments on the manuscript, and especially her constant reminders that a theoretical argument needs a 'kitten', an example as concrete as a little cat, to illustrate what's meant.

We have always enjoyed and appreciated the collegial spirit, enthusiasm and professional insights of the IRC licensees, who have helped to launch the approach in different parts of the world, and who have generously shared with us their ideas on practical applications and ways of giving constructive feedback to respondents from different cultures and countries.

Our appreciation also goes to our clients, and the participants of our programmes, who have been curious to learn more about assessing and developing intercultural competences. Their feedback and practical comments have been extremely valuable to us, and have given us new ideas for how to combine competence assessment with intercultural learning and development programmes.

Ever since we started our work as intercultural consultants, we have benefitted greatly from working with Fons Trompenaars and Charles Hampden-Turner. Thanks to their creative thinking, wit and inventive contributions to the field, the close cooperation in particular between Oscar, Fons and Charles has enriched our understanding of intercultural management development. We have always enjoyed our conversations with them about how we could support our clients in benefitting from their diversity and developing sustainable solutions for a global workforce.

Prior to working as intercultural consultants, we had the privilege of learning from some outstanding individuals. In particular, we would like to thank Alexander von Bormann, Norbert Groeben, Wolfgang Klein, Willem Levelt and Ralf Nüse for their academic rigor and creativity, their integrity and fun-seeking curiosity. Ursula's special thanks go to Melissa Bowerman, who would have read this book with her distinctive mixture of scepticism and inquisitiveness.

Introduction

A couple of years ago we were teaching cross-cultural management to MBA students at an international business school when a student came up to us and said, 'It's been an interesting class, but you have to hurry up in making money, because you will be out of a job soon.' When we asked him why, he said that the cultures of the world are becoming more and more alike. Wherever he travelled he would find the same type of hotels and the same type of food; the people he met were all connected to the internet and all looked forward to the launch of the next version of the iPhone.

In some deeper sense he was right. Anthropologists like Wade Davis have been warning us that more than half of the 6000 languages spoken around the world today are at the point of disappearing,[1] that our cultural diversity is diminishing much more rapidly than our biological diversity. Perhaps some of us are tempted to welcome this development, secretly hoping we all end up speaking English – a language we've mastered already. How inconvenient for most of us if for some mysterious reason that last language turned out to be Tzeltal. It would force us to struggle finding words for all the concepts and ideas that currently shape our experience of reality; leaving us lost in translation, sensing that our new vocabulary never quite expresses what we wanted to say, never being certain whether what we said resonates with our hearers.

In this book we will share with you our experience of working with companies, business schools and universities on the topic of dealing with cultural diversity. The fundamental questions behind much of our work have been: are you looking at the world around you to find similarities and to confirm what you already thought? Or do you feel that what you experience as your world is not an objective fact, accessible to all normal people, but just one of the many models of reality? To what extent do you allow for the idea that there are many different interpretations of the world around you, that cultural diversity is a source of creativity and innovation, reflecting the ingenuity of the human mind, inviting us to imagine alternatives?

People who have realized this are incredibly effective when working across cultures – and when working with people from their own culture. Why do they connect so well with very different people around the world, why do they deliver results where others have failed, and why do they draw so much energy out of working with people from other parts of the world?

Their talent is to imagine alternatives. Our goal is to translate this talent into intercultural readiness.

Why We Wrote this Book

Our world needs cross-cultural talent. Countries have never before been so open for business from other countries as they are today. But many companies are baffled and shocked to find that their staff – their executives – cannot deal constructively and openly with their counterparts from other cultures. They lose business because of misunderstandings; they lose profit because executives do not understand how things are done in India, China or Nigeria.

When we set up our cross-cultural consulting firm in the mid-1990s, rapid expansion of trade across the world was just beginning. 'Culture' was a hot topic, and many businesses initially thought they needed lists of local custom and practice – clink your glass below your host's in China; don't ask after your colleague's wife in Dubai; say 'Bonjour' when entering a shop in France.

Our background was in psychology, linguistics, philosophy and business anthropology, and we quickly realized that while this kind of cross-cultural training was useful, it did not tackle a basic fact: some people seem naturally gifted to connect across cultures, effortlessly engaging people from other cultures and winning their commitment for working together. We set out to explore what this talent consisted of, what these people were doing that others were not doing. And the better we became in formulating what worked, the more enthusiastic we became about supporting people in developing these skills.

With the help of psychologists and anthropologists, and of many people with a skill and background in international business, we started to develop a method for assessing one's intercultural competences – a series of interlocking skills and attitudes that influence how a person deals with people from other cultures.

We were excited to discover just how we could support people in developing the competences they lacked, and encourage them to work with those in which they were stronger.

The Intercultural Readiness Check: Assessing Intercultural Competences

The **Intercultural Readiness Check** is a questionnaire that these present authors have developed in consultation with internationally renowned, cross-cultural psychologists in the dominant universities in the field.

By assessing their intercultural competences with the Intercultural Readiness Check (the IRC for short), people learn what they do well already, how they can use this to support the process of intercultural interaction, and how they can develop those areas that need improvement. The IRC assesses a linked series of four intercultural competences, which contribute to working more effectively across cultures. These competences are Intercultural Sensitivity, Intercultural Communication, Building Commitment and Managing Uncertainty, and they will be described in more detail in the chapters that follow.

We developed the IRC in 1999, and initially brought it into use in 2001, after two years of research and development with input from leading psychologists at the University of Groningen.[2] One of the first valid and reliable intercultural assessment tools on the market, it has been constantly refined and improved over the course of 12 years.

Since 2003, more than 400 intercultural professionals have become licensees. They work from the United States to China, from Australia to Brazil, from Ireland to Russia, and from Norway to South Africa. The licensees vary from human resources departments in multinationals to academics performing research, and from educational institutions working with international students to companies training candidates for intercultural work. As people from all around the world have used the IRC, through our own work with them, and through the work of IRC licensees, we have continually reassessed the quality of the questionnaire at regular intervals, with the help of cross-cultural psychologists from universities in Groningen, Amsterdam, Ghent and Toronto.

In 2009, we issued a major re-analysis of the IRC, which at that time included data from more than 10,000 respondents. The outcome suggested that we could improve the measurement of three competences with some small changes. But we also decided to make bigger changes to improve the scale assessing one particular competence: Intercultural Communication. We defined new questions to assess this competence, and tested them until we were certain that they worked together to form a scale. With this we had a better tool than before, again with four strong scales.[3] This new version of the IRC has been in use since 2010.

To date, the IRC has helped more than 30,000 individuals to become more effective when working with people from other cultures. When participants fill in the questionnaire, their answers are compared to those of thousands of people who have used the IRC before them, allowing them to compare their own approach to intercultural interaction with those of many others who have been facing similar challenges, and in particular to learn from those people who have a real talent for intercultural interaction.

How Do Intercultural Competences Develop?

This book sets out some of the most important insights from our research on intercultural competence assessment and development.

For the analyses presented here, we have included the data collected up to 31 December 2012. By that date, 27,290 people from some 400 organizations and over 170 countries had answered our questions for assessing Intercultural Sensitivity, Building Commitment and Managing Uncertainty, and 12,250 people had answered our questions assessing Intercultural Communication.

All these people had also answered questions about their biography and background, the number of languages they speak, how much time they had lived outside their home country, and their status in their work (this status measurement based on how many people directly report to them). Approximately 22,000 respondents described their attitude toward working internationally, and more than 4300 respondents told us how they feel about diversity and working in multicultural teams.[4]

We have analysed this enormous databank with advanced statistical techniques to learn more about how talent translates into intercultural competences. How do intercultural competences develop – do we see a steady increase, or rather leaps forward in development? Can people lose competences that they have developed? What is the impact of having lived in other cultures, how do age, management level and speaking foreign languages contribute? Are women better interculturally than men, or vice versa?

We were also able to explore how culturally diverse teams benefit from interculturally competent team members, and whether the four different competences assessed by the IRC contribute differently to the success of a culturally diverse team (they do). We were able to discover whether some companies had more interculturally competent staff than others, and why this might be so. And it was possible to test whether some groups see more value in diversity than other groups. As we were using the IRC in our work with clients, we constantly looked for new ways to use this IRC data for research and theory development.

Our method has been used by numerous organizations and individuals from around the world, and their answers have been brought back, anonymized and fed into the developing research. The IRC, our assessment tool, is now a standard method for assessing, developing, refining and training intercultural readiness.

In this book we will share the findings that we discovered on this journey.

How this Book is Organized

In Chapter 1, *Intercultural Readiness: Translating Talent into Competence*, we introduce our Intercultural Readiness approach to intercultural effectiveness. The Intercultural Readiness approach works with four intercultural competences, offering clients a clear structure for becoming more effective across cultures, that is, to better connect to people from other cultures, perform more effectively and efficiently in achieving task-related goals, and find intercultural interaction more enjoyable.

Chapter 2, *Why We Need Intercultural Competences*, addresses the popular hope that to do business across cultures, all we need is information about them. Request for such information often reflects true interest in another culture, and the desire to avoid offense and show respect. We will argue that the request for information about other cultures may lure people into a false sense of security. It may keep them from facing the emotional challenges that come with learning about cultural differences, from accepting the need to learn about themselves, and to change because of what they learn. Reliance on knowledge alone keeps them from developing the competences they need. Intercultural interactions are complex, their outcome often unpredictable. To be interculturally effective, we need intercultural competences.

Chapter 3, *The Four Competences*, describes how the four intercultural competences support people in effectively working and relating across cultures. Drawing on our own research, and on findings from psychologists, linguists, communication researchers and leadership experts, we will show why these four intercultural competences are vital for anyone who is working across cultures. Real-life examples and case studies from global organizations will illustrate just how these competences have helped people to become interculturally effective.

Chapter 4, *Different Talents, New Abilities*, shows how we use the IRC feedback to support people in their competence development. For each competence we will show how people who have developed the competence can contribute to the process of intercultural interaction; how those who lack it can temporarily compensate for the gap by focusing on other competences, and how a sole reliance on one competence can keep them from developing all competences.

Chapter 5, *Intercultural Competences Develop by Themselves: True or False?*, critiques the belief that intercultural competences develop all by themselves through exposure to other cultures. From the curriculum in schools to the people companies choose to work abroad, this exposure equals competence belief is deeply ingrained in the logic of our training, selection and development systems. But it's wrong. Intercultural competences do not grow and blossom through exposure to other cultures. In fact, exposure may have made your global professionals less competent than they were before going out into the world.

Chapter 6, *Intercultural Competences for Culturally Diverse Teams,* looks at why culturally diverse teams can fail so dramatically in achieving their performance goals. But they can benefit from their differences, and outperform less diverse teams, if they get a grip on their process. We will show which attitudes and competences help teams to get a grip on the process. Teamwork is hard, and there is a limit to what a single interculturally competent team member can do to make it easier. By assessing all team members on the four IRC competences, organizations can determine how much support their teams need for getting a grip on their process and achieving all their performance goals. A seven-point action plan will give you a hands-on tool for supporting your culturally diverse teams from start to finish.

In Chapter 7, *What Makes an Organization Interculturally Competent?*, we move from the team context to the organizational context. We will share with you our findings on how successful diversity management enables people to develop their intercultural competences. Diversity management is hard, and many good initiatives have failed. A study on the diversity perspective that works, and on those that don't work, we found to be particularly helpful in understanding what is needed. Standing on the shoulders of giants is a good position for an outlook.

Effective diversity management brings the strongest advocates of diversity into key positions, who in turn will support their organization in enabling individuals and teams to develop their intercultural competences. Intercultural competences may very well be the linking pin between an organization's success in going out into the world, and letting the world come in.

chapter 1

Intercultural Readiness: Translating Talent into Competence

We are all foreigners now. Working life entails some degree of intercultural interaction for most people today: a French investment manager from a development bank visiting start-ups in Africa; an American kindergarten teacher educating children whose parents have brought them from Pakistan; a Brazilian leading tax partner rapidly putting together an international team for a global audit.

And thousands of organizations operate across national borders. In 2011, more than 300,000 US companies engaged in international trade; two years earlier than that, Germany had close to 110,000 exporters and importers. There are a stunning 56,834 international NGOs operating in 300 countries and territories.[1]

World universities offer study-abroad programmes to 2.8 million students; the National University of Singapore alone lists 180 partner universities in 33 countries. The United States hosts close to 40 million immigrants, while the United Kingdom has sent out three million expatriates. Foreign workers account for almost 90 per cent of the population in the United Arab Emirates, and close to 70 per cent in Kuwait.[2]

Even in the tiniest place, internationalization is apparent; the authors of this book recently overheard locals outside a bar in a German village, exchanging tips on dealing differently with Dutch, Polish and Estonian truck drivers.

The Need for Intercultural Readiness

Many industries and companies now see substantial economic growth only outside their traditional home base. Doing business across borders is no longer an additional option – it is the only way to create a sustainable future.

Organizations operating globally are now very aware that culture matters. They know that their customers, staff, suppliers and other stakeholders may have widely varying expectations, needs and preferences because of their different cultural backgrounds. And they have learned that cultural differences can be like a tripwire, waiting to catch them at a vulnerable moment and wreck their chances. These organizations know that they need to understand cultural differences and take them into account in their business dealings.

But it is one thing to know that cultures differ, and another thing altogether to decide what to do differently because of it. Take the case of two bankers who were sent from the United States to Asia to lend money. This was a very important deal: if things went right, this loan would fund a private company that was committed to creating sustainable growth in its country and enhancing the living conditions of its workers.

The two bankers were expecting to meet one, or perhaps two, senior people who would have the ultimate say in negotiating the loan and its terms. But when they arrived at their destination expecting to be shown into a quiet office, to their shock they instead found themselves facing 27 people around a boardroom table.

How were they to deal with this, they wondered; should they shake hands with all 27, then find out who were the two money men they should be talking to and somehow dismiss the other 25? After all, they were here to talk to the people who knew the details of contracts, and who had responsibility for borrowing and paying back.

This is where intercultural readiness comes in; that readiness to respond openly and constructively to an intercultural challenge. Intercultural readiness is not about playing games, to cunningly mirror others' body language and speech so as to trick them into trust; it's not learning how to game the system. It is about understanding, communicating and cooperating with people from other cultures just as effectively and honestly as one does with people from one's own culture. And it always involves learning about ourselves.

One of the key aspects of intercultural readiness is the ability to stay flexible and alert in dealing with other cultures – and to have faith that people with different ways know what they're doing. This is what the two bankers did. They sat and talked, and listened. And gradually it became apparent that all 27 of the people facing them would be affected by the proposed borrowings, all needed to know that they were dealing with trustworthy people, and to see what deal was on the table. The two young bankers were flexible and open; they behaved impeccably towards the 27 new customers and, after a while, most of the 27 gradually excused themselves with thanks and drifted away, leaving the final two who would take responsibility for the nitty-gritty of the financial deal to sort things out and sign the papers.

Interactions like this, which hold such risks of misunderstanding and cultural clashes, are why many organizations are no longer satisfied with learning about cultural differences. Instead, they are looking for tools and approaches that help their staff to translate information about cultural differences into new ways of working with people from other cultures. The key step to achieve this is to define the competences that people need for working effectively across cultures.

The present authors began work in the area of intercultural management development by training people in understanding and managing cultural differences. As we worked with an increasing group of clients from every continent and many cultural backgrounds we came to realize that there are core intercultural talents and competences that can be identified, trained and developed. We worked with internationally experienced psychologists, organizational consultants, senior human resource professionals and intercultural trainers from five different cultures in developing a method to assess these intercultural competences, and to identify and improve competences in individuals and in workgroups.

The system that emerged, and which has been refined over almost 20 years of development, we call the **Intercultural Readiness** approach.

Intercultural Readiness: An Interlocking Set of Competences

Intercultural readiness is a mindset, and it is a core requirement for all staff dealing with people from other cultures. As we worked with an increasing number of managers and executives, in our intercultural training courses in international negotiation for global professionals, we realized that intercultural training required a two-sided approach. First, it was necessary to thoroughly understand participants' work context and performance requirements, and how these are affected by cultural differences. Second came the work of spelling out the attitudes, ways of thinking and behaviours that would help participants to achieve their goals in their cross-cultural work environment. By defining the attitudes, ways of thinking and behaviours that support effective intercultural interaction, we built a compact but rich set of interlocking intercultural competences.

The approach that we developed works with four competences that are naturally linked to the process of intercultural interaction. Each competence has its own subset of abilities.

These are the four basic competences of our approach to intercultural effectiveness:

Intercultural Sensitivity captures how much people are interested in what makes people different because of the culture they come from; it also indicates how much we are willing to take into account the fact that our own culture has formed us, and that people from other cultures have been formed differently. Intercultural Sensitivity supports the first step in intercultural interaction, where we need to explore our differences.

Intercultural Communication assesses how flexible we are in expressing ourselves, and how mindful we are when communicating with people from other cultures. This competence is essential for managing the second step in an intercultural interaction, where differences need to be addressed in appropriate ways.

Building Commitment enables people to build strong relationships that survive tensions and conflicts, and to focus on new solutions that work for all parties, which in turn strengthen the relationship. Building commitment is vital for the third, and perhaps most complex, part of the interaction, where we need to agree on a shared approach.

Managing Uncertainty is the ability that allows people to stay alert and creative throughout the interaction process – rather than stopping exploring their differences, falling back on their automatic ways of communicating and seeking a quick fix through old solutions. Throughout the process of intercultural interaction, we need to handle uncertainty. Differences may unexpectedly pop up, our partners in a negotiation may suddenly fall silent and we don't know what to do about it. It may take a lot of good thinking, and more time than we thought we had, to create new solutions to shared problems. The interaction itself, and its outcome, will often be uncertain, with no simple solution suggesting itself.

These four intercultural competences come into play whenever people from different cultures interact, whether they need to negotiate with foreign government officials, recruit and motivate talent in their different locations around the world, create high-performing virtual teams, or create momentum for their diversity agenda. In all these situations people need to understand different viewpoints and needs, adapt how they communicate, create commitment around shared goals and stay in charge when situations become uncertain, confusing and unpredictable.

Learning from the Talent of Others

Everyone has a unique profile of skills and talents. How to develop those you have, and improve or work around those you lack – that is the secret of intercultural readiness.

A shipping company, for example, regularly sent engineers to Hong Kong for meetings with their local provider to review the ship management. Initially those meetings were frustrating. The engineers sat across from the company's general manager, flanked by three technicians on each side. The engineers explained what they wanted to see improved. The general manager agreed to the suggestions. But nothing happened afterwards.

This changed only when a new and culturally talented engineer joined the team. He immediately sensed that the general manager lacked the technical expertise to evaluate the engineers' suggestions – his role was to represent the firm. The general manager had been pretending to understand the complaints so as not to lose face, and so had agreed to make improvements that were unfeasible. His technicians had the expertise, but since their boss had already agreed to the impossible they could not disagree and suggest alternatives. But they could not do what their boss had promised either and so nothing had ever been done.

The culturally gifted engineer changed things so that the engineers learned to use the formal meeting just for pleasantries and to address their issues with the technicians in private afterwards. The situation changed – now, the technicians and the engineers found solutions to the problems together, and the technicians could implement what was agreed.

That engineer's cultural intuition came from a natural talent – that intense and acute sensitivity to our own dealings with others that we call Intercultural Sensitivity. In analysing what people talented in this area do well, we identified a set of behaviours and ways of thinking that can be practised and developed by those who are less talented in this aspect but who are able to develop the competence.

The four competences of the Intercultural Readiness approach, and how they are connected to the process of intercultural interaction, provide a clear and simple structure for learning and development. Through focusing on these four intercultural competences, it is possible to learn from the talents of others, and develop one's own skills in dealing constructively with intercultural challenges.

Intercultural Competences and Intercultural Effectiveness

In our work on intercultural competence development, we have found it useful to distinguish between intercultural *competences* and intercultural *effectiveness*.[3] Intercultural competences are a means to an end: these competences are needed in order to be interculturally effective – that is, to solve problems and achieve objectives together with people from other cultures. Which competences are needed, and to what degree, depends on the problems that need solving and the objectives we want to achieve together with others.

For a call centre agent in Mumbai servicing US customers, for example, intercultural effectiveness may include staying on top of US local news and knowing how the Red Sox are doing in the World Series. This requires rapid intake of new information and the intercultural sensitivity to quickly assess whether the customer on the other end of the line is interested in baseball or thinks of it with disdain.

A Swedish jazz composer, coming from a country where compliments are only given in cases of outstanding excellence, may need to learn to compliment his fellow performers at the Berklee College of Music in Boston more often. This requires intercultural communication skills, and in particular an understanding that in the US, compliments are a strategy for reducing social distance between him and his musicians, making his team feel comfortable and acknowledged so that they perform at their best.

An economist from New York may have to learn to be less direct when discussing next year's budget with her Bostonian boss at Harvard. This again requires intercultural communication skills, but also the ability to build commitment, and to manage the uncertainty that results from her personal feeling that her Bostonian boss is being arrogant.

While problems and objectives determine which intercultural competences are needed – and to what level – intercultural effectiveness always requires paying heed to three criteria:[4]

- connecting to people from other cultural backgrounds,
- performing in achieving task-related goals, and

• enjoying the pursuit of common goals in a culturally diverse environment.

In our work, we focus both on the intercultural competences that support the process of intercultural interaction and how these competences contribute to intercultural effectiveness.

Often, people in business just focus on performance, and underestimate the need to build relationships with people whom they do not know very well yet. But their ways of building relationships may differ, and while people may approach each other with the best possible intentions, they may misunderstand these intentions and feel puzzled, disrespected or even offended. Working with people who are like us is comfortable; we feel reassured and confirmed in our ways. But when we are with people from other cultures, we may be in doubt about what they are thinking, how we should behave. We need to stay alert all the time and constantly pay attention, and this is difficult. Interculturally effective people have learned to keep track of how much they are enjoying the interaction, and take their own personal and professional needs seriously.

When we work with business and academic clients who want to become more effective in their intercultural work environment, we ask them what they want to improve in their work with people from other cultures. Their answers are always straightforward – within seconds they tell us that they want to better connect with others, or to perform more effectively and efficiently, or to enjoy their intercultural work more than they do at present.

By distinguishing between intercultural competences and intercultural effectiveness, people checking their competences can first decide what they want to improve – whether they want to improve their relationships with others, perform better or feel more comfortable in working across cultures. We then bring in the feedback on the IRC scores in the individual competences to help them better understand their existing approach, and how they can improve it to achieve the goals that are important to them.

Exercises

1) Make a chart, showing the four intercultural competences managed in the four corners: Intercultural Sensitivity, Intercultural Communication, Building Commitment and Managing Uncertainty. Ask your family to tell you a story about yourself illustrating your skill in each one.

2) Tell a funny story concerning another cultural group. Now think about telling the same story to a member of that cultural group. Would it be funny to that person? Discuss this mentally with yourself. Score yourself from 1 to 5 on how much you have learned by switching perspective.

3) Gather together a team of four people from different cultures – whether these are national cultures or different cultures of other sorts, like married actors and teenage boys, atomic scientists and baristas – to play a game of table tennis. Encourage them and coach them to make them a great team for that hour or two. Score how well this diverse group has built its commitment.

4) Go somewhere that you are sure to meet complete strangers whose culture is foreign to you: a country & western bar if you are an opera aficionado; a CoderDojo programming class if you are great at DIY but only know computers as a magic box. Try to be nice and pleasant and not come across as a dork. Measure the amount of cold terror-sweat you produce. How good are you at Managing Uncertainty?

Key Points

- Defining and developing intercultural competences is a response to organizations' growing need to have staff competent to work across cultures.
- Intercultural readiness is based on four interlocking **competences** that reflect the process of intercultural interaction:
  o **Intercultural Sensitivity**, which captures how much we are interested in what makes us different because of the culture we come from,

o **Intercultural Communication**, which assesses how flexible we are in expressing ourselves, and how mindful we are when communicating with people from other cultures,
o **Building Commitment**, which enables us to build strong relationships that survive tensions and conflicts, and
o **Managing Uncertainty**, which allows us to stay alert and creative throughout the interaction process.

2

Why We Need Intercultural Competences

Over the past 20 years, more and more organizations have begun to select and develop staff based on thoroughly assessing them on relevant competences. Competences enable individuals to show exemplary performance and to respond to new and changing organizational challenges. With job demands becoming more complex and unpredictable, job-specific knowledge quickly grows outdated. In searching for individuals with the right competences, organizations strive to attract and develop professionals who know how to adapt their approach when faced with new and unforeseen demands.[1]

The intercultural profession has seen a similar trend from knowledge transfer to competence development. As the search for global professionals intensified, discussions of 'intercultural competence' increased along with it.[2] Yet while organizations now commonly assume that job-specific knowledge is no longer sufficient for mastering today's demanding jobs, when it comes to mastering intercultural challenges, many people still assume that knowledge about other cultures alone will make them interculturally effective.[3]

This reliance on cross-cultural knowledge is one commonly held misconception about what makes us interculturally effective. Another common misconception is that to interact with people from other cultures, it is best to focus on what we have in common and to downplay what makes us different.⁴

While we need both cross-cultural knowledge and similarities to effectively interact across cultures, neither of them is enough. Instead, we need to develop specific intercultural competences in order to manage the process of intercultural interaction and to respond to new and unforeseen intercultural challenges.

Knowledge Does Not Equal Appropriate Behaviour

Knowledge of other cultures is important. To work with people whose customs and norms are different, we need to know what those customs are, and understand their norms. But knowledge alone doesn't make us effective.

A simple example showing the limits of knowledge is the taboo in countries like Malaysia and Indonesia on eating with one's left hand. The left hand is reserved for personal hygiene, which makes it very offending to use that same hand for eating and passing objects to other people. This information is easy enough to take in and remember. But putting the knowledge into practice is very hard for left-handed people, who use the left hand for moving objects and the right hand for steadying them. A left-handed manager once told us that even after 20 years in Asia, he still has to literally sit on his left hand when having dinner with friends and business partners from countries where the taboo holds – since otherwise he would break the taboo that he knows exist and start eating with his left hand. (See Box 2.1 for another example.)

BOX 2.1 DINNER IN TOKYO

In 1992, a Scottish scientist was invited to Japan with a group of colleagues. He was well-read on Japanese customs, and thrilled the others with his explanations of the inner workings of shrine symbolism, business card rituals and the correct depth of the bow. But when it came to actually interacting with the Japanese, he was quite insensitive to customs and expectations. The group was invited to dinner by their Japanese hosts, and as soon as the guests were served with their bowls of noodles, he picked up his chopsticks and fished around underneath the noodles to discover what lay beneath.

'There's always something lurking under Japanese food,' he explained to the mystified Europeans. Their hosts' smiles froze.

The Japanese were very uncomfortable. He had ruined the chef's arrangement, and in showing off his knowledge he had put them in a horrible position – insulting the chef of the exclusive restaurant they had selected, and insulting his hosts in ignoring their culture's dedication to style and beauty.

A culturally competent person might have known about the custom, but he would have also been attuned to the people around him, listening and watching carefully, sensing when to show delight at the delicious surprise, and when to share his cultural knowledge.

We Never Know Enough about Another Culture

Cross-cultural knowledge is not enough for being effective because we may encounter situations where people behave in ways that we could not possibly predict, based on what we know about their culture. We once watched a Japanese movie about a school experiencing serious issues. One teacher in particular seemed to be responsible for this. The movie features a young girl as heroine who dares to openly protest against the situation. Her protest culminates in her publically scolding – in the presence of all other students, their parents, the director and the entire teaching body – the oldest teacher of her school! Even us hardy folks from less face-sensitive cultures felt sorry for the man. The scene goes against everything that can be read about the Japanese respect for status, how respect is particularly due to older people and teachers, and how mortifying it is for people to be criticized in public. Breathlessly we watched how the entire audience in the movie applauded the girl. To understand the scene, one needs to understand the values that were at stake which legitimized the young girl breaking all these norms of polite and respectful behaviour in Japan that any informed foreigner knows by heart. When we discussed the scene with our Japanese colleague Masako Kato, who did not know the movie, she suggested that for such a scene to be plausible, the teacher being scolded must have done something that had harmed the entire community of people involved with the school.[5]

Believing that knowledge about another culture alone will make us effective when interacting with people from that culture will lull us into a false sense of security. The belief will shut down our ability to observe, to take in contradictory information and to search for cues from others about how best to respond. We need to search constantly for new information if we want to understand what is truly going on in any particular intercultural situation. Of the intercultural competences in the Intercultural Readiness approach, it is Intercultural Sensitivity that is most relevant for dealing with this part of the intercultural interaction process – where we need to explore our cultural differences.

Learning New Behaviours

Knowledge about other cultures doesn't suffice for being interculturally effective – we also need to behave differently. The need for acquiring new behaviours is particularly evident when it comes to intercultural communication: how do we give feedback, hold a presentation or instruct people to do something? All these behaviours need to be adapted, and new behaviours learned depending on the culture(s) we are dealing with. Expanding our behavioural repertoire tends to take time and practice, which is illustrated by the example in Box 2.2.

BOX 2.2 DINNER IN AMSTERDAM

A Dutch company acquired a French company. For once, it seemed, the Dutch had done everything right. In contradiction to the famous stereotype that tells us that Dutch people find it hard to part with their money, the company reserved a table in one of the finest restaurants in Amsterdam.

During the dinner the most prestigious French wines were served accompanied by a joking explanation of Dutch directness and French indirectness. By midnight the French had started singing – usually a good sign.

Unfortunately, however, this was the moment when the Dutch financial manager could no longer control his need to be direct. All evening he had been watching the party somewhat sceptically, but after the first three songs he felt the moment had come to bring up the subject he had been waiting to discuss all evening. He turned to the French CEO and said: 'I have been looking at your financial figures today, and I feel there's a lot you will have to explain to me tomorrow.'

The French team fell silent, finished their Grand Cru and started to look at their watches. A whole evening ruined by dreadful timing.

It is one thing to know that most French are more indirect than most Dutch, and to play along with this different communication style for a while. It is quite another to be satisfied with hours of rapport-building and indirect communication.

How quickly can we translate an awareness of culturally different communication styles into a gut feeling of trust that the other party also knows there are issues to be addressed, and that rapport-building and indirect communication increase our chances of actually resolving these issues together?

Intercultural competences deepen our understanding of a situation. If you know that the French management team will address important issues more cautiously and at a different time, how comfortable are you with this? How able are you to switch your behaviour without losing track of important issues? How well can you seize the opportunities that present themselves in a different, indirect way to make your points and, most importantly, how do you build on an indirect style to be more effective when you need to be direct?

In the example of the Dutch–French dinner, described in Box 2.2, the key to effective intercultural communication is an intuitive sense of timing. Let's assume for now that French business people often prefer to build rapport rather than discuss the company's balance sheet while having dinner. This does not mean that they keep focusing on food, wine and rapport-building the next day. Instead, the rapport that has been built over dinner provides a basis for addressing more confrontational topics later on, and to explore these confrontational topics in much greater depth and openness than without having built that rapport.[6]

What matters during intercultural interaction is not just what we know about each other, but how we use our knowledge, how we manage ourselves when our habits are strong, what we do when we don't know enough, and how easily we can acquire new behaviours. These learning needs can only be addressed by focusing on intercultural competence development.

Focusing on Similarities Does Not Make Us Interculturally Effective

But is it really necessary to focus so much on cultural differences? To get along with colleagues and business partners from other countries, shouldn't we better concentrate on what we all have in common instead of getting stuck on what makes us different? Questions like these often reflect a sincere intention to relate to people from other cultures, to be fair and respectful in how we interact with them. But while we need to work skilfully with our similarities to initiate and build relationships, we must also acknowledge our differences.

Pretending there are no differences does not make us feel closer to one another, it doesn't help us to be more accurate in perceiving where each of us is coming from, and it doesn't help us to acknowledge and appreciate that other people may have other goals and values. This is the message from recent work on colour-blind versus multicultural attitudes, which was initiated by psychologists Christopher Wolsko, Bernadette Park, Charles M. Judd and Bernd Wittenbrink, with their study, 'Framing Interethnic

Ideology: Effects of Multicultural and Color-Blind Perspectives on Judgments of Groups and Individuals'.[7] A 'colour-blind' attitude reduces our ability to accurately perceive, evaluate and behave towards people who come from different ethnic groups. The experiments conducted by Christopher Wolsko and his team are described in more detail in Box 2.3.

BOX 2.3 A MULTICULTURAL ATTITUDE IS MORE EFFECTIVE THAN A COLOUR-BLIND ATTITUDE[8]

Which attitude works best for achieving harmony between different ethnic groups in a country – a colour-blind or a multicultural attitude? Christopher Wolsko and his team wanted to know which of these two perspectives would be more effective in promoting harmony between ethnic groups in the United States. In a series of experiments, white US American students were assigned to three different conditions. In the colour-blind condition, students were encouraged to consider what all people have in common at their core, that men and women are created equal and that, first and foremost, the US is a nation of individuals. Students in the multicultural condition were encouraged to appreciate the diversity of the different ethnic groups in their country, and that each group has positive as well as negative qualities. Students in the control group were not specifically instructed to think about harmony between ethnic groups. How would the students be influenced by the different instructions – colour-blind, multicultural and control – in how they felt about, perceived and judged their own and other ethnic groups?

The results of the experiments were unequivocal: taking a multicultural perspective on achieving harmony between ethnic groups is better than taking a colour-blind perspective or not being reminded at all of the need to achieve harmony between groups.

Students who had been encouraged to adopt a multicultural attitude were better in identifying and acknowledging that different ethnic groups may have different values and principles guiding them in their life, and may live in different social realities. They were more willing to acknowledge existing stereotypes rather than pretending that such stereotypes do not exist. In acknowledging stereotypes, students in the multicultural condition had also become more balanced, that is, they considered both the positive and negative aspects of the stereotypes of all groups, their own and other ethnic groups. Importantly they were also more accurate in assessing which assumptions commonly made about the different groups were actually correct. When predicting the likely behaviour of fictitious people from various ethnic groups, students instructed to take the multicultural perspective were more precise than the other two groups in that they integrated the unique information about the fictitious individuals with information given about the ethnic group to which the fictitious characters belonged.

On all measures – feelings, perceptions, judgements and prediction of behaviours – students who had been encouraged to appreciate the diversity of the different ethnic groups in their country were better able to respond to this reality than students in the colour-blind condition, who had been instructed to focus on what all people have in common at their core.

The studies by Christopher Wolsko and his team show that we need to acknowledge our cultural differences. What helps in doing this is realizing that we all have multiple cultures within us; for example, our new colleague may be an Estonian, but also a visual artist, Muslim, brought up in Ireland and a passionate skier. Reflecting on these multiple cultures, how would you describe your cultures? In how many ways could **you** find similarities **and** differences with this new colleague?

People who are interculturally competent can find commonality among their own multiple cultures, and the other's multiple cultures, inviting the other to explore what they have in common without ignoring the differences.[9]

Focusing on similarities alone does not help us to manage the interaction nor to achieve our goals – we will miss critical information and reach only a shallow mutual understanding. But neither will we succeed if we only look at one way of being different, for instance how our national cultures or religions differ – since then we will only see differences: differences between two large, internally homogeneous groups.[10] Intercultural interaction then easily turns into a win–lose power play, fuelled by fear of one-sided adaptation and mounting frustration of not achieving our goals.[11]

Building Commitment around Shared Goals

To be interculturally effective, we need to build commitment around shared goals, and to agree on how to move forward. We may convince the other to do what we had in mind, we may adapt to the other's goals, do nothing or compromise, or we may together change our minds and develop better goals.[12] The ability to build commitment creates opportunities for testing different approaches, and to build on each other's ideas in order to identify new space for problem-solving (see Box 2.4 for an example). Through building commitment, our own values can be enriched if we allow ourselves to be confronted with values that at first may seem the very opposite of our own values.[13]

BOX 2.4 BUILDING COMMITMENT FOR SAFETY MEASURES

An example of understanding and working with two conflicting values comes from the story of a European steel company that was asked to modernize a steel factory in Mexico. One of the main concerns was to create a safer work environment.

For the European management team, safety standards were non-negotiable. Their company did everything from developing very sophisticated technological solutions to enforcing standards to providing training, education and assistance ensuring a safe and healthy workplace. During their first visit to Mexico, the management team was unimpressed by a presentation on the health and safety regulations of their Mexican counterparts. The standards were far lower than those acceptable in Europe.

Worse still, when they later talked to some of the steelworkers, they discovered to their dismay that even these insufficient regulations were mostly not taken seriously. Many of the workers said that, ultimately, life and death were in God's hands. The way to ensure safety, they told the European managers, was to go to church every Sunday and pray for divine protection.

It was a delicate situation. The European management team was sensitive to the cultural orientations that were at play here.

A less sophisticated team might have described the steelworkers' position as totally unacceptable, and pressurized the local management team to implement European safety standards.

This team chose a different approach, realizing that they were dealing with two completely different value orientations: the European belief in safety as a joint responsibility of management and shop floor; and the Mexican steelworkers' fatalistic belief that they were in the hands of a higher power.

Brilliantly, the European management team ignored obvious solutions – and turned to the local church. They found that the church leaders were also deeply dismayed by the lack of good safety practices – especially because injured workers were treated in church hospitals and they saw the havoc caused by lax safety practices.

The church leaders agreed to join in the safety presentations, signalling that safety in work did not rely entirely on faith, but also required safe work practices. Safety regulations did not deny the need for the protection of higher forces, but instead showed gratitude for their concern for you.

The effect was revolutionary: the number of accidents began dropping immediately, and the safety record of this factory became a boast. The leaders' response to the safety dilemma showed how much leaders of international organizations need the ability to build commitment, and how much they can benefit from it if they invest in this ability.

In the example of European safety standards and Mexican religious standards described in Box 2.4, the members of the management team were competent in many ways, but most of all they demonstrated the ability to build commitment. They took the needs of the Mexican steelworkers seriously, showing genuine respect for a culture foreign to them, and so managed to solve a seemingly intractable value conflict.

When the European management team returned, they took home from their experience in Mexico the knowledge that health and safety issues would be managed even after people had left the company premises.

This led in turn to a cultural change in the Europeans: through this experience, the management team became much more active in partnering with city councils, hospitals and other parties who also took an interest in the health and safety of employees, and those affected by their actions.

Managing Our Energy

To interact effectively across cultures, we need to focus much more on the other party than we do when interacting with people who share our cultural routines. But we also need to be aware of ourselves. How long do we feel comfortable outside our comfort zone? How long can we tolerate gaps in knowledge and routines yet put our best foot forward? In intercultural interactions, we need to stay alert, monitor what we say and how we behave. Numerous studies have shown that our energy to do this is limited. Our self-control battery may run out of power, and we may experience what is called ego depletion – when our ability for self-control vanishes like air from a balloon (only usually without the squeaky wail).[14]

Ego depletion temporarily reduces our capacity or willingness to engage in further self-control, to make rational choices, to initiate and monitor action. We simply need a break (ideally, with chocolate).[15]

When does it hit us? This depends on how much a person enjoys the uncertainty of intercultural interactions.[16] To probe yourself in this area, ask yourself: when I am with people who act very differently from myself, do I feel anxious and stressed or energized and eager to learn more? When my expectations again and again are not met by the other culture, do

I become curious or annoyed? How long can I enjoy the surprise, and when do I need to take a break because I've had enough surprises for the day?

If we lose track of how much energy we have left, ego depletion will hit us. We may say the wrong things, cause havoc and justify the outcome by blaming 'them'. And this may very well be the end of our intercultural learning adventure.

Senior Executives Know They Need Intercultural Competences

Out of our database of 30,000 business people, 1651 are senior executives with more than 50 people working for them. About a third of them score very high on our Intercultural Readiness Check competence measure, Intercultural Sensitivity, while about a quarter of them score rather low on Intercultural Sensitivity.

When answering the IRC, most of these senior executives were also asked how well they could perform in a job that requires intercultural interaction. Of the interculturally sensitive executives, 75 per cent said they had no doubt whatsoever that they could perform well in such a job. In contrast, of the executives who had not yet developed their Intercultural Sensitivity, less than 25 per cent felt fully capable of performing in such a job.

We also asked them how comfortable they feel when interacting with people from other cultures. More than 65 per cent of the interculturally sensitive senior executives said they felt absolutely comfortable interacting with people from different cultural backgrounds. In contrast, among the executives who had not yet developed this competence, less than 25 per cent said they felt fully comfortable interacting with people from other cultures (see Table 2.1).

Table 2.1 shows, for executives with more than 50 people reporting to them, the relationships between their Intercultural Sensitivity scores, their belief in their own ability to perform across cultures and their sense of comfort when interacting with people from other cultures.

Table 2.1   Relationship between Intercultural Sensitivity scores, beliefs about own performance and sense of comfort with intercultural interaction among executives

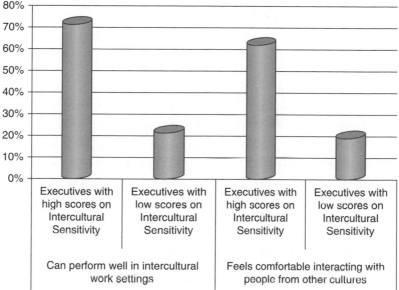

It is safe to assume that most of these executives are responsible for an organization, or substantial part of an organization, that operates across borders – why else would they have taken the time to assess their intercultural competences? Their answers to the IRC reveal that senior executives are struggling, just as many other people are, when it comes to the intercultural part of their job. A quarter of the senior executives in our database score low on Intercultural Sensitivity, a competence that is crucial to grasping the size of their cross-cultural business challenge. Apparently many senior executives still need to come to grips with the consequences of operating globally, with the impact that cultural differences have on their organization's potential for success (see Box 2.5 for a case study example). But their answers also show that senior executives are keenly aware that they can only perform in their cross-cultural job, and feel comfortable dealing with people from all those different cultures, if they are interculturally competent.

BOX 2.5 CASE STUDY: CREATING CONNECTIVITY
THROUGH DIVERSITY

Ralf Schneider, MD, Better Business (2B)

Ralf Schneider, Managing Director of Better Business (2B), founded PricewaterhouseCooper's Ulysses program in 1998. The global services powerhouse saw the coming of an internationalized world, and moved to train its executives in a different way of working. Ulysses became a byword for getting people ready to deal with an international job environment.

'In PwC, international collaboration is of the essence,' says Schneider. The firm had to hire and groom high-level staff who could work across boundaries – cultural, functional, departmental boundaries, as well as those between industry sectors. 'The ability to work and operate across boundaries is the essence of the value proposition – if you can't cross boundaries, there's no value in your network,' he says.

But how do you create that connectivity? You can create it through processes, systems, products and marketing propositions. 'But at the end of the day it's through people working together on a cross-boundary, cross-border basis. And diversity is the starting position for this.'

PwC created the Ulysses program, sending teams of young executives to developing countries to help with specific problems. But while the young managers thought this was all about their success, it was, very importantly, also about their way of working together – they were there to learn a new way of working.

At first, the executives going on schemes to tackle AIDS in African countries and get rid of landmines or reintegrate combatants in strife-torn nations were all Anglos. However PwC discovered fast that the scheme gave more value in many ways if they mixed the teams.

And rather than the executives coming back with knowledge of other cultures, the ones who became real leaders had become interculturally competent: building relationships across cultures; valuing people of different cultures; coping with ambiguity;

listening and observing; translating complex information; managing others, taking initiative, adapting and managing stress.

In one case, three executives came back from Vietnam thinking that they had done a perfect job because they had fulfilled their task. But they had rammed through their plan without consultation. As possible candidates for promotion, they'd dropped down the ladder.

'Maybe this is because many executives who make it to top levels have followed a specific management education, one that fosters a control mindset. People who have learned to succeed with that mindset first feel extremely uncomfortable to go into another environment. And people do this in international management; the more they think they're in control, the more value they destroy.'

In one project Schneider describes as 'magical', a Dutch, a Mexican and a Canadian completely changed their way of operating as individuals: 'It was a mindset shift, caused by the needs of problem-solving in a complex environment. Leadership in that environment meant stepping out of the way, stimulation, encouraging people – and when they went back to their home teams, they now operated in a completely different way.'

It is a constant problem for companies that people posted abroad often leave the posting around the two-year mark. Schneider points out that this may be a career choice: 'These people have stepped back into line, because that's how the career system works. There are all kinds of reasons for people to stick to their knitting and not expose themselves in terms of international mobility and exposure and immersion into other cultures.'

But he also notes that the type of people who love the travel, exposure, learning and finding out new things, have or develop a mentality that is perfectly poised and trained for leadership: 'It's a mindset to think in terms of dilemmas; with that mindset you step out of your comfort zone into new territory, expose yourself to new learning, keep yourself curious, loving complexity and using it as a source of growth and learning.

In many ways it's the same mindset that drives entrepreneurs: people who like to operate at the edge, rather than on the safe patch where it becomes competitive. In many ways this is a leadership mindset.'

chapter 3
The Four Competences

The competences that are key to successfully interacting with people from other cultures build on the skills we use when we interact with people from our own culture, in our careers and personal relationships. But these *intercultural* competences are more than general interpersonal skills: they demand of us that we constantly anticipate how cultural differences may be affecting our interaction, and that while we look for similarities between us and the other in order to build common ground, we must neither ignore our cultural differences nor forget that the people involved come from different groups and cultures.

Each of these competences faces two ways, like the head of Janus, the Roman god of transitions, whose statues guarded the entryway of homes, one face looking alertly outwards, the other watching inwards to the courtyard and the living rooms.

The four Intercultural Readiness Check (IRC) competences, Intercultural Sensitivity, Intercultural Communication, Building Commitment and Managing Uncertainty, work in tandem, each with these inward-looking and outward-facing facets. Table 3.1 shows what these are, and how they work.

The four competences and their facets are about reflecting how we differ from others, and also about continually testing our current assumptions

Table 3.1   The four IRC competences and their facets

INTERCULTURAL SENSITIVITY	
The degree to which we are actively interested in other people's cultural backgrounds, their needs and perspectives.	
Facet 1: Cultural Awareness The ability to see our own interpretations, norms and values as culture-specific, and to consider different cultural perspectives as equally valid.	**Facet 2: Attention to Signals** The extent to which we seek information about others' thoughts and feelings by paying attention to verbal and nonverbal signals when interacting with them.
INTERCULTURAL COMMUNICATION	
The degree to which we actively monitor how we communicate with people from other cultures.	
Facet 1: Active Listening The degree to which we are mindful when communicating with others, and pays due attention to their expectations and needs.	**Facet 2: Adapting Communicative Style** The degree to which we adjust how we communicate in order to fine-tune a message in line with cultural requirements.
BUILDING COMMITMENT	
The degree to which we actively try to influence our social environment, based on a concern for relationships and integrating people and concerns.	
Facet 1: Building Relationships The degree to which we invest in developing relationships and diverse networks of contacts.	**Facet 2: Reconciling Stakeholder Needs** The degree to which we seek to understand the interests of different stakeholders, and can create solutions to meet these needs.
MANAGING UNCERTAINTY	
The degree to which we see the uncertainty and complexity of culturally diverse environments as an opportunity for personal development.	
Facet 1: Openness to Cultural Diversity The degree to which we are willing to deal with the added complexity of culturally diverse environments.	**Facet 2: Exploring New Approaches** The degree to which we are stimulated by diversity as a source of learning and innovation, and risks trying out new ideas.

and checking what other strategies might work in the current situation. Through their two-sided nature, each competence allows us to interpret the data coming in to us from others, whose background may be different from ours, whose culture may be foreign to us, whose signals may be unfamiliar or misleading to us. And each also allows us to reconfigure our own signals as they go outwards to others, so that we suit our signals and actions to the other party's cultural filters, expectations and needs.

People who lack these competences may find themselves mysteriously blocked in their career advancement as their company expands abroad. They may be unable to attain key positions after their company merges with a competitor. As entrepreneurs, they may fail to grow their business in foreign markets.

But people who have developed these competences connect to foreign business partners and learn about their unique business interests. They ignite culturally diverse teams to perform beyond expectations. They contribute to their organization's efforts to benefit from diversity.

Each of the four competences and their facets affects our intercultural interactions in different ways, and, through continually strengthening them, we become more effective in our dealings with people from other cultures.

Intercultural Sensitivity

Intercultural Sensitivity is a measure of how actively we are interested in the needs and perspectives of people from other cultural backgrounds. People who are interculturally sensitive thoroughly analyse how expectations and needs may differ, and this analysis in turn leads them to constantly attend to verbal and nonverbal signals.

It is a key ability when we are checking whether we know enough about a given situation. For instance, a student who has joined a class in a new country may find that her fellow students start the project work quite differently from the way she expected – energetically creating presentation slides with ideas about possible solutions rather than first calmly establishing an agenda of who needs to achieve what at which point in time. If she is interculturally sensitive, she will allow herself to try out this unfamiliar approach and compare it to the one she knows well. If she is closed off, she will think *'Project work without an agenda? All mad!'* and insist on doing things the way she has learned to do them back home.

The first facet of Intercultural Sensitivity, **Cultural Awareness**, indicates the extent to which people reflect on their own culture and consider other cultural perspectives as equally valid. People who score high on this facet continually generate multiple interpretations of an event, and use these interpretations to reflect back on their own way of doing things.

Being able to use different cultural perspectives for making sense of someone's behaviour is the essence of cultural awareness. Doing so also helps us to see our own behaviour through the lens of someone from a different culture. Take the case of a young Chinese psychologist, who gave an excellent presentation at Stanford University. At the end, he thanked his professors for their help – these professors being the two grand ladies of the field. He laid it on thick by western standards, though from a Chinese point of view he was merely acknowledging how deeply he was indebted to them as supervisors of his PhD research.

Looking at this story, and reading his behaviour from the two alternative cultural perspectives, enables us to realize how our own actions – perfectly readable to those who share our cultural background – may be perceived quite differently by others. To the westerners listening, he appeared to be fawning on his professors; to those of his fellow-students from China, he was modestly giving credit and gratitude where it was due. Which leads to the question: when showing appreciation to a Chinese business partner in the usual understated western way, might we come across as uncaring and rude?

The second facet, **Attention to Signals**, indicates to what extent people seek information about others' thoughts and feelings. By paying close attention to verbal and nonverbal signals, people who score high on this facet constantly check whether their interpretation of an event is correct. An interculturally sensitive negotiator can pick up signals that others fail to notice, and so realize factors that are not apparent to those lacking intercultural sensitivity, as illustrated by the case in Box 3.1.

BOX 3.1 ATTENTION TO SIGNALS IN CROSS-CULTURAL NEGOTIATIONS

An example of a negotiation that had gone very wrong, but was rescued by a negotiator sensitive to unfamiliar cultural signals, was one in which a UK purchasing team was buying T-shirts from a supplier in Pakistan. The suppliers were eager for business, and the UK purchasers were tough enough to push the Pakistanis for the best price possible. What the purchasing team did not realize was that the money they were offering was below the price at which the supplier could afford to produce the T-shirts.

When it came to delivery time, the samples of T-shirts arrived in the wrong colour. There was a lot of discussion, with the buyers saying 'Sorry guys, we agreed on this,' and the suppliers 'Our machines are not able to produce this colour.' The British were frankly stymied. They could not understand why colour was suddenly part of the equation.

Then a new member of the buying team joined the UK side. This was a man who was very attuned to cultural signals. During his very first conference call, he noticed what the others had been missing all along – the signals of distress in the suppliers' voices. He realized immediately that the problem had nothing to do with colour. The price the Pakistani suppliers had been forced to concede was simply beyond their capacity, and they were now trying to sell the company T-shirts in the wrong colour, in the hope of getting an order for something else, something they could afford to supply.

He nudged his colleagues to end the call, and once the suppliers were off the line, he explained the situation. When the UK team called back, they readily renegotiated the price. Now, of course, the suppliers said the T-shirts could be produced in any colour – because they could afford to produce them.

When people score high on both **Cultural Awareness** and **Attention to Signals**, they are able to make these two facets of Intercultural Sensitivity work in tandem. High scorers continually generate more than one interpretation, and check which interpretation seems most plausible given the signals they receive. They can create a much more accurate idea of what drives others' behaviour than people scoring low on these facets.

Why is Intercultural Sensitivity Important for Intercultural Effectiveness?

Studies by psychologists and business specialists overwhelmingly show the importance of intercultural sensitivity for those working with people from different cultures.

In his 1989 publication, 'A Study of Cross-Cultural Effectiveness: Theoretical Issues, Practical Applications', Daniel J. Kealey examined 12 challenges expatriates have to deal with, for example, adjusting to the new environment and transferring technical skills. Kealey found only a single cluster of competences that consistently correlated with effectiveness in all 12 areas, a cluster comprising empathy, respect and tolerance – skills and attitudes that are core elements of intercultural sensitivity.[1] More recently, psychologists Regina Hechanova, Terry A. Beehr and Neil D. Christiansen showed, in their 2003 publication 'Antecedents and Consequences of Employees' Adjustment to Overseas Assignment: A Meta-Analytic Review', that expatriates who could accurately understand the feelings of others found it easier to adjust to their new environment than those who could not empathize well with others.[2] In their 2005 meta-analysis of 30 studies, 'Predicting Expatriate Job Performance for Selection Purposes: A Quantitative Review on Personality Factors Predicting Expatriate Job Performance', psychologists Stefan T. Mol, Marise Ph. Born, M.E. Willemsen and Henk T. van der Molen identified intercultural sensitivity as one of the strongest predictors of expatriate job performance.[3] Many other studies have demonstrated how vital intercultural sensitivity is for intercultural effectiveness.[4] It is not surprising then that psychologists David C. Thomas and Stacey R. Fitzsimmons concluded in their 2008 literature synopsis, 'Cross-Cultural Skills and Abilities', that *'empathy or intercultural sensitivity (in its various manifestations) seems to be one of the most robust predictors of effective intercultural interaction'*.[5]

Given the overwhelming evidence that intercultural sensitivity contributes to intercultural effectiveness, it is astonishing that our research shows that scores on this competence do not currently correlate with managerial position. If companies systematically assessed intercultural sensitivity when deciding whom to promote to managerial positions, we would expect to find people in higher management positions to have higher average scores on our IRC measurement of Intercultural Sensitivity than people in positions with lower managerial responsibility. But, as shown in Table 3.2, average scores on Intercultural Sensitivity are roughly the same across all levels within an organization.

Given the critical role of intercultural sensitivity for intercultural effectiveness, we recommend that all companies working internationally, and all with a cultural mix among their workforce, assess staff to see how they score on this competence, and, in particular, assess those staff members who are aiming for international roles.

Table 3.2 shows the average results (with a minimum of 10 and a maximum of 50 points) for Intercultural Sensitivity for five different groups of respondents, for a total of 27,181 respondents. Worryingly the management levels show virtually no difference in competence.[6]

Table 3.2   Intercultural Sensitivity and management position

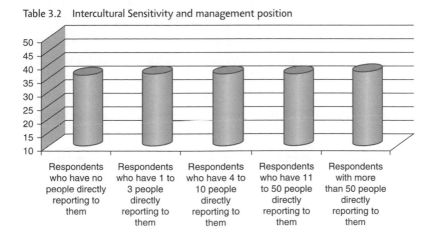

Respondents who have no people directly reporting to them	Respondents who have 1 to 3 people directly reporting to them	Respondents who have 4 to 10 people directly reporting to them	Respondents who have 11 to 50 people directly reporting to them	Respondents with more than 50 people directly reporting to them

Intercultural Communication

Intercultural Communication is about establishing meaningful dialogue, where both parties' needs and perspectives are equally valid, and both are responsible for preventing and repairing misunderstandings.[7] It requires listening closely to what the other party is trying to say, expecting throughout that our perspectives may differ. It also requires adapting how we try to get our message across. The two are connected: if we focus only on adapting, but not on the perspective of our listener, we fail to notice that what is so evident to us may not be clear to the other. Intercultural Communication is the key to building common ground.

Developing this competence is a challenge. This is illustrated by the story of a colleague of ours, Viviane, a US trainer working for a large multinational corporation. Viviane was invited to give a training session in Shanghai to a group of Chinese colleagues. She knew a lot about Chinese culture and customs, and was keenly aware that Chinese people are extremely sensitive about loss of face.

Viviane was determined to adapt her style to avoid causing loss of face. But Viviane was haunted by a nightmarish thought – that her colleagues would invite her to a restaurant where she would be served dog. She loved dogs, and had two dogs of her own – the thought of eating dog was unbearable. Viviane tried to indicate her concern indirectly when introducing herself at the beginning of the training. She talked about herself as a person, and about her family, and she showed a picture of her dogs, telling her audience how much she loved them. She must have gone on with her subtle plight for just a bit too long. Suddenly, one of her participants raised his hand and said, 'Don't worry, Viviane, we won't serve you dog. It is summer now, and dog is a winter meal!'

Monitoring how we communicate is like having a camera on our shoulder that gives us online feedback on how we come across when we speak, how the other may have understood what we tried to say, and how else we may need to formulate our message.

In the two facets of Intercultural Communication, we distinguish between a more receptive and a more active component – **Active Listening** and **Adapting Communicative Style**.

Active Listening indicates how much attention we pay to the other's expectations and needs. Take a look at this exchange during a business trip in Thailand:

Passenger to taxi driver: 'How far is it to the airport?'

Taxi driver to passenger: 'Do you need to wash your hands?'

To make sense of the exchange, you have to engage in active listening. The passenger in the exchange was baffled by the driver's seeming non sequitur – but for the tactful Bangkok driver, it seemed obvious that the passenger was too embarrassed to say directly that he needed the toilet.

People who are skilled in active listening take more time for communicating than people who are not so skilled, and routinely consider multiple interpretations of what the other makes of the exchange. To communicate at all, we must be able to listen actively to some degree. But high scorers do this more often, and more consistently, than people who score low on this facet.

The second facet, **Adapting Communicative Style**, captures how well we fine-tune our communicative behaviour in line with cultural requirements. Take a look at Box 3.2 for a case in point.

BOX 3.2 ANGER MANAGEMENT ACROSS CULTURES

An impressive example of adapting communicative style comes from an intercultural conference we attended in Konstanz. As we came downstairs into the lobby of our hotel we heard a British guest in a wrinkled shirt complaining loudly. The legendary

British stiff upper lip was notably absent – he was complaining furiously to the receptionist that, contrary to promises, there was no iron in his hotel room and actually nowhere in the entire hotel. How was he to enjoy his conference dinner, sitting next to colleagues in a shirt like his? He seemed out of his mind with anger.

We were fascinated – during the opening gathering the night before, we had heard Peter Franklin, Professor of Intercultural Communication at a university in the town, mention how British people had to become more direct if they wanted to be heard when making complaints in Germany.[8]

When the man in the wrinkled shirt sat down next to us at the dinner table, we asked him about the encounter – and when he just smiled, we continued, 'With all these cultural differences on how we show emotions, how angry were you on a scale of 1 to 10?'

He shrugged and replied, 'I'd give it a "1". I am an actor, I know how to do this.'

Why are Both Facets of Intercultural Communication Relevant?

Global organizations today increasingly seek to hire local recruits rather than sending home-country managers on costly expatriate missions. Job interviews in which applicant and interviewer come from different cultures (see Box 3.3) are typical examples of situations where cultural differences can obstruct mutual understanding, and where active listening and adapting our communicative style are vitally important.

BOX 3.3 ADAPTING OUR COMMUNICATIVE STYLES IN JOB INTERVIEWS

To prevent misunderstandings in international job interviews, recruiters, applicants and the management of the hiring firm need to understand their different assumptions about how people present themselves in such an interview.

A European multinational wished to hire a senior executive for its Indian organization, and engaged an executive recruitment firm to find suitable Indian candidates. Following initial interviews with the finalist candidates in India, the two best candidates were brought to Europe for interviews with top management. One candidate remained, but the management team hesitated – they doubted whether this man would be assertive enough to meet the demands of this top managerial position.

The candidate displayed verbal and nonverbal behaviours that caused the European management to have some doubts, and so he was perceived to be submissive rather than assertive and confident. When debriefing the interview with the recruiter, the management's bias became clear. The candidate had been showing respect in ways that were entirely appropriate for an interview by higher management in an Indian context. This was a clear case of cross-cultural misunderstanding. But the story had a happy ending: the recruiters explained the cultural dissonance to the multinational's executives, and the candidate got the job, and performed superbly in it.

Self-Presentation Style Depends on Context

In their research on impression management in job interviews, psychologist Marianne Schmid Mast and her team from the University of Neuchâtel found that Swiss job applicants may have a hard time convincing recruiters from Canada of their suitability for the job. The Swiss culture values modesty and team orientation. Canadian recruiters, in contrast, come from a culture that emphasizes more individualistic values; for example, being unique and outstanding, and making yourself heard.[9]

In their 2011 study, 'Self-Promoting and Modest Job Applicants in Different Cultures', Schmid Mast and her team had an actor impersonate a modest candidate for some interviews, and a self-promoting candidate for others: and, as expected, they found that Canadian recruiters were much more interested in hiring the actor when he portrayed a self-promoting candidate than when he played a modest one. To Canadian recruiters, the self-promoting style signalled competence, while modesty was interpreted as lack of competence, and it was this inferred competence that influenced their interest in hiring the candidate.[10]

In cross-cultural job interviews, both interviewer and applicant benefit from active listening in assessing whether their expectations about self-promotion are aligned. Applicants can manage the impression they want to make through adapting their communicative style to the culture-specific expectations of recruiters and interviewers.

If you wonder whether you tend to undersell yourself, take a look at Table 3.3 with our advice based on the work by Schmid Mast and her colleagues to see how you could adapt your style to leave an indelible impression on your audience.

Numerous studies have analysed how cultural values influence how we communicate. Across studies, two key factors have been identified as critical for how directly we make our point:

- The extent to which we focus on being clear and effective, focusing on the task at hand[11]
- The extent to which we focus on differences in power and status, and on the people involved.[12]

We may have learned to be direct because our culture taught us to be clear and effective; but we may also be direct because our culture emphasizes power differences, and we happen to occupy the power seat. Cognitive psychologists Ute Fischer and Judith Orasanu's highly instructive article, 'Error-Challenging Strategies: Their Role in Preventing and Correcting Errors', captures six ways in which we can give instructions, which range from a very direct to a very indirect way of telling another person what to do.[13] Table 3.4 illustrates these six ways of giving instructions – from very direct to very indirect.

Table 3.3   Modest style as opposed to self-promoting style in interviews[14]

	Modest style	Self-promoting style
Verbal indicators	Do you tend to present yourself as undemanding, as someone who does not consider themselves a person who outperforms other potential applicants?	Show that you are confident, sure of your personal values and ready to convince the recruiter that you are the best match for the job profile.
	Do you explain your failures by lack of talent and effort, but your successes by luck and ease of task?	Explain your failures by ill fortune and undesirable circumstances, and your successes by your superior talent and intelligence.
	When asked why you once quit a job after a short while, do not say: 'Well, how should I put it, we decided that I did not completely match the job profile?'[15]	Say: 'I had the impression the job profile did not meet my expectations and ambitions.'[16]
	Do you use disclaimers (for example, 'I don't know'), hedges (for instance, 'Isn't it?'), filler words like 'umm'?	Don't. Speak fluently instead. You will also save time.
	Do you hesitate when answering?	Answer questions swiftly and fluently.
Nonverbal indicators	Do you lean tensely forward in your chair?	Assume a relaxed posture.
	Do you nod a lot, and fidget on your chair?	Nod less, stop fidgeting.
	Do you avoid eye contact?	Meet the interviewer's gaze.

Table 3.4   Six ways of giving instructions*

Instruction	(Please) Call the client and make an appointment.
Obligation	We need to call the client and make an appointment soon.
Suggestions	Let's go call the client and make an appointment.
Queries	How about getting in touch with the client?
Preferences	I think it would be wise to get in touch with the client.
Hints	We haven't been in touch with the client for some time now. (Also known as 'the baby is crying' strategy.)

*Based on Fischer and Orasanu, 'Error-Challenging Strategies: Their Role in Preventing and Correcting Errors'. Adapted with permission by the authors.

Listening actively is critical for mutual understanding when our cultural backgrounds differ with respect to task orientation, or with respect to how we deal with status differences. A manager's indirect instruction (for example, 'We haven't been in touch with the client for a while.') may be taken as an interesting comment by a task-oriented assistant (who might think 'Yes, that's true.') or as embarrassingly meek by subordinates accustomed to unambiguous orders ('Why is my boss talking to himself all the time?'). A direct order would be more effective in these situations, for example, 'Please phone the client and find out if she needs us to send more products.'

Research into cockpit communication has theorized that when captain and co-pilot were not aligned in status, or when cockpit crew and tower crew were not aligned, planes have crashed.[17] The work of Ute Fischer and Judith Orasanu on cockpit communication shows how communicative training can help cockpit crew to communicate more effectively, especially in emergency situations.[18] Their work is an excellent example of how intercultural communication professionals can support their clients in understanding the sources of their cross-cultural misunderstandings.

Active listening and adapting our communication style are essential if we wish to communicate effectively across cultures. Earlier work on cultural differences in communication may have overrated some of the nonverbal differences, for example, the time we take before we respond to a speaker.[19] Recent studies by a research group at the Max Planck Institute for Psycholinguistics in Nijmegen suggest that *all* cultures base their timing on the rule of *no gap, no overlap* when taking turns in speaking (and that not even the famously taciturn Scandinavians wait longer than 200 milliseconds before responding).[20]

Other nonverbal differences may have been misinterpreted, for example, how we use eye contact in informal settings to regulate whose turn it is to speak. A study published in 2009 by linguists Federico Rossano, Penelope Brown and Stephen C. Levinson, 'Gaze, Questioning, and Culture', suggests that in informal settings speakers' eye contact does not vary as much across cultures as has long been assumed. Speakers of languages as different as Italian, Mayan Tzeltal (Mexico) and Yélî Ndye (Russel Island, Papua New Guinea) – places that are 14,000 kilometres apart from each other – can all make hearers respond faster by looking at them when they are done speaking. Eye contact by hearers, in contrast, does differ: for Mayan Tzeltal, for example, hearers tend not to look at the speaker, while for Yélî Ndye and Italian, hearers look freely at the speaker to signal that they are ready to speak now.[21] Empirical research on cultural differences in nonverbal communication may still hold its surprises for theorists of intercultural communication.

But the research on job interviews, the examples in Tables 3.3 and 3.4 and Fischer and Orasanu's analyses of cockpit communication leave no doubt that we must be able to adapt our style both in terms of what we say and how we say it, if we want to be effective communicators in today's culturally-mixed world of work.

Building Commitment

Building Commitment is about engaging people in a constructive and creative problem-solving process, based on an understanding of the other's different needs. Through relationships with a range of people who differ from us, we can solve problems better and faster than people who have a narrower, less diverse range of contacts. To do so, however, we have to violate Law Number 1 in psychology, 'similarity attracts', because to do so we need to draw energy from people who are not like us.

An Australian mining company invested into Building Commitment when they invited leaders of the Aboriginal community to a week-long, cross-cultural training programme. Instead of only listening to presentations on Aboriginal culture and beliefs, participants could now learn from Noel Pearson, Aboriginal Australian lawyer and land rights activist, about what the company's mining activities meant to the Aboriginal community; and they could talk and discuss this with the Aboriginal representatives for several days during the programme and over dinner afterwards. This intense exchange with members of the Aboriginal community gave the mining company's staff a much deeper understanding of, and respect for, the community's needs and concerns about the land than would have been possible through a more traditional cross-cultural training programme.

The intercultural competence Building Commitment captures the degree to which people actively try to influence their social environment, based on a concern for relationships and integrating different people and perspectives.

Its first facet, **Building Relationships**, is how much we invest in relationships and in developing diverse networks of contacts. Even introverts can find this fun.

Building relationships isn't always done in an obvious way. For instance, a senior manager for a financial services firm in Hong Kong found it difficult to get the right contacts with key decision-makers – until he convinced his company to buy him a Ferrari. This enabled him to join the Ferrari Owners' Club of Hong Kong, a powerful network of business people and entrepreneurs. His contact list grew at accelerated speed – and he was happy driving a Ferrari.

By becoming a member of different groups, we become familiar with using different codes, practising different roles and taking on different identities. Groups regulate membership through implicit and explicit codes, like wearing the right sneakers to show you are in the know, or wearing shirts with cufflinks rather than buttons to signal your status.

Knowing the code is essential for a group of expatriates in Amsterdam who meet on Saturday afternoons in a tiny wine shop hidden in the basement of a narrow house in the Grachten quarter, just off Rijksmuseum. Each expatriate brings a bottle of wine wrapped in aluminium foil to hide the label. The challenge is to bring wine that will surprise the others – just bringing very expensive wine would testify to an embarrassing lack of finesse and show that you didn't know the code implicitly agreed by this group.

The more we choose to be only with one type of people, the more we are determined only by their cultural code. We may become suspicious of people with different beliefs and even avoid contact with them – much like cousins of ours who were warned by their Catholic grandmother not to play with Protestant children.

When we build diverse networks, we start to understand the meaning of different cultural codes, and become comfortable in making the connections between them – discovering, for example, similarities between the code of avoiding boasting among Dutch people, and the code of modesty women often use when responding to each other's compliments.[22] We also become more aware of the effect that different collective customs have on ourselves, more self-confident in choosing between them, and in accepting or ignoring the code.

The second facet of Building Commitment, **Reconciling Stakeholder Needs**, keeps us focused on what we can achieve together while at the same time strengthening our relationships through constructive problem-solving.[23] A high-tech company we've worked with used this approach for product innovation. The company hired many creative people who would constantly approach their management with ideas for new products. The executives had to decide which of these ideas should be accepted, but often had to take care of daily business and had no time to carefully evaluate these ideas. The company did not want staff to argue forever about whether a rejected idea should in fact be accepted, but they could not risk losing brilliant ideas either.

To solve the dilemma, they installed the Box of Rejected Ideas: all staff members could submit their rejected ideas to the box, and at intervals the management team would open the box and give the rejected ideas a second chance. This worked so well that many of the company's key innovations came out of this miracle box.

Building Commitment is Vital for Global Leaders

For effective global leadership, Building Commitment is the most important of all the intercultural competences. This competence is far more strongly developed by senior managers in organizations than by people

Table 3.5   Building Commitment – a competence developed by executives

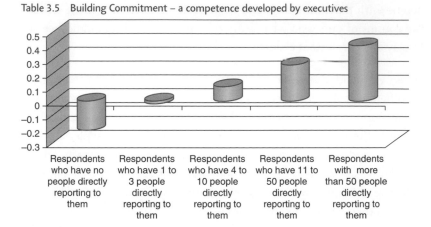

Respondents who have no people directly reporting to them	Respondents who have 1 to 3 people directly reporting to them	Respondents who have 4 to 10 people directly reporting to them	Respondents who have 11 to 50 people directly reporting to them	Respondents with more than 50 people directly reporting to them

Table 3.5 shows the findings for Building Commitment for five different groups of respondents. The results, showing standardized scores (see Box 3.4), are based on answers from 27,181 respondents from five different management levels, with higher scores reflecting higher levels of competence.

without managerial responsibility (see Table 3.5); our IRC data reveal a significant correlation between Building Commitment and management level.[24]

BOX 3.4 STANDARDIZED VERSUS AVERAGE SCORES

Table 3.5 uses standardized (standard) scores rather than average scores to show the different competence levels between the five groups. Standard scores capture more information than average scores, because they take into account how **typical** a single respondent's result is given the results of **all** respondents. Ultimately, the goal is to test how consistently a given group shows the measured behaviour. This is achieved through statistical techniques that first capture how all individual results are distributed along the answering scale and then calculate how typical each individual result is compared to all results.

In effect, each of the 27,181 individual results is first weighed in terms of how extraordinary, how rare or how common it is, given all results, and only then are these weighted individual results added up to calculate the five different group scores. The resulting standard scores for the five groups therefore reflect more precisely the differences between the five groups than the groups' average scores. One outcome of all these calculations is that the standardized group scores now range from minus 1 to plus 1, with the average result now being expressed as zero. Positive scores show that a group's results are above the average of all 27,181 respondents, while negative scores show that the group scores fall below that average.

Scoring high on **Building Commitment** means that people score high on *both* its facets, **Building Relationships** and **Reconciling Stakeholder Needs**. This score reflects a global leadership mindset. Effective global leaders acknowledge and appreciate the complexity and ambiguity of the context within which they operate, and continually strive to respond constructively to this complexity, knowing that they cannot rely on the same solution for a long time. They do not seek the comfort and safety of a homogeneous network, nor do they pick and choose different cultural collectives, moving in and out of them like frequent flyers through airport lounges.

Instead, to establish and maintain their networks, and to reap the benefits of their diversity, effective global leaders approach value differences and conflicts flexibly. They are driven to create reconciled, integrated solutions when faced with seemingly opposing cultural orientations. Leaders are successful in building large networks when they understand the needs and interests of different members of the network, and are able to create flexible solutions to meet those needs. This takes a strong awareness of value differences, and it is here that the two facets work most clearly together.

People who are less successful in building diverse networks very often see tensions in their network in terms of good or bad, professional or unprofessional, trustworthy versus untrustworthy. They see one set of values as desirable and everything that looks like contradicting these values as undesirable. One set of ideas is seen as creating value, whereas other ideas are seen as destroying value. Their solution to conflict is 'my way or the highway' – much like a company owner who does not allow staff to work from home because he or she fears they won't actually work unless they are in the office.

Effective global leaders go beyond this notion. They understand how different ideas can create value for different members of the network – they see their ultimate challenge in intergrating the value orientations of the different stakeholders in their multiple diverse networks. In Box 3.5, we discuss Building Commitment in the context of current leadership theories.

BOX 3.5 BUILDING COMMITMENT AND LEADERSHIP THEORY

The competence Building Commitment can best be understood as the extension of effective leadership into a global context. Current leadership theories have moved away from a perspective within which leaders have specific 'leadership qualities', which allow them to function from a well-defined leadership position in a clear and predictable hierarchical system.[25]

Instead, current work on leadership (for example, Bernard M. Bass and Bruce J. Avolio's work on transformational leadership, and the Complexity Leadership Theory developed by Mary Uhl-Bien, Russell A. Marion and Bill McKelvey[26]) strives to capture the complex context within which leadership is needed, and to describe leadership in terms of changing roles, relationships and processes that need to be managed for achieving organizational goals.

This view of leadership has to some extent discarded the notion that a given person is and will always be the leader, due to inherent and unique leadership qualities. Instead, researchers now focus on how leadership takes shape within a network of human interaction.[27]

One approach to leadership, called the Leader–Member Exchange (LMX) approach, for example, analyses the two-way relationship between leaders and those in their team. LMX theories focus on how leaders develop an exchange relationship with each team member, and on how the quality of the relationship in turn influences behaviour, effort and loyalty towards the leader.[28]

'Leader-follower' relationships often create an in-group of team members, who are close to the leader and trusted by him or her, and an out-group, who are kept at arm's length in terms of influencing, decision-making and access to resources. Leaders tend to include people in their in-group who are similar to them – that is, those of the same gender, from the same cultural, professional or ethnic background.

The key challenge for global leadership is to overcome this bias towards similarity. We have found that the ability to build commitment develops at all levels of management through substantial experience abroad, allied with friendship across cultures, and that as Building Commitment develops, people increasingly commit to diversity and overcome the similarity bias.

Among the relationship-focused leadership approaches, social network theories of leadership highlight the broadest array of relationships to be considered for effective leadership. In their 2006 article, 'The Ties that Lead: A Social Network Approach to Leadership', management expert, Prasad Balkundi, and organizational behaviour specialist, Martin Kilduff, set out to close 'the gap at the heart of our understanding of leadership'. Balkundi and Kilduff emphasize that in order to be effective, leaders need to accurately perceive the networks that surround them, and know how to influence others through understanding the social dynamic within these networks.[29]

If social networks are as decisive for today's leadership as Balkundi and Kilduff and others argue, then interculturally savvy people will have a head start in effective leadership. People who are interculturally competent avoid the downsides of a strong and cohesive ego network – the network immediately surrounding the leader.[30] Cohesion in this inner circle, powered by perceived similarity and the pressure to conform, strengthens the clique but clogs the channels through which new and fresh information flows.

People who can build commitment are particularly resistant to preferring those who are like them over those who are different, and so are particularly skilled in keeping open the channels that connect them to a wide range of opinions, supporting new and creative approaches.

Managing Uncertainty

Managing Uncertainty is a game-changer. Do we seek to be with different people, get to know different groups, explore different ways of doing things because it invigorates us? Or does this leach energy from us, because dealing with people who think and act differently makes us feel uncertain, stressed, suspicious, alone and at a loss? Managing Uncertainty is about learning how cultural differences can energize us, so that we are ready to continue developing our intercultural competences.

An example indicating the need to develop this competence is that of a software developer who was used to following precisely the instructions of her boss, and so felt most comfortable when she could be absolutely sure about what was expected of her in any given work situation. When she relocated to the country in which her company's head office was based, she worked with colleagues who valued personal initiative and knowing when to make an exception to the rules set by their managers. But each exception meant uncertainty for her, risking imperfection and disobeying her boss. She needed a lot of time to let go of her need to follow the rules exactly, and to trust herself that she would learn when to make the right exception.

This competence identifies the degree to which we see the uncertainty and complexity of culturally diverse environments as an opportunity for learning and personal development. People who manage uncertainty well enjoy the uncertainty that comes with a culturally diverse context, seeing it as a constant source for learning and development.

Managing Uncertainty differs from the other IRC competences in that it does not offer a well-defined starting point from which we can expand our skill range slowly and steadily. For the first three competences of the Intercultural Readiness approach, learning entails taking stock of what we do well already and building on this. Developing our Intercultural Sensitivity, for example, starts with reflecting on our own cultural approach. Improving our Intercultural Communication skills means looking at our dominant communicative style and practising styles that are less typical in our culture but more dominant in other cultures. Improving our skill in Building Commitment starts with understanding our own values, then exploring the other party's values with the goal of creating solutions that integrate both value orientations.

Unlike these intercultural competences, Managing Uncertainty requires us to take a leap of faith into the unknown. Cross-cultural encounters may be disorienting at times – comparable to the sensation of a European tourist in Australia who tries to find her way back to the hotel after a copious dinner in the Barossa Valley, only to realize that there is no North Star shining home. We need to manage ourselves when experiencing the uncertainty of cross-cultural encounters, staying curious and willing to learn – even if we have lost sight of our cultural coordinates.

The first facet of Managing Uncertainty, **Openness to Cultural Diversity**, reflects how much we are willing to deal with the added complexity of a culturally different or more diverse environment. Imagine you just arrived in Tokyo for the very first time. You are hungry and want to buy a sandwich in a supermarket near your hotel. The shelves hold hundreds of neat, transparent boxes with colourful pretty content – but is it edible? Is it fish or vegetable, sweet or sour, with or without additives, should we eat it hot or cold, for breakfast, lunch or dinner, and what about our allergies? The labels are not helpful either – they only show black and white drawings. Do you take the box with the prettiest colours or do you opt for room service back in your hotel?

Or imagine a professor from Japan who is used to students showing respect for her achievements by not confronting her or asking difficult questions during class. Teaching at a university in the US may be quite a challenge at first, since now students may openly disagree with what she has to say – not a sign of disrespect from them, but a sign that they are sparked into investigation and intellectual interest by her scholarship. Cultural differences can challenge us in many ways, but the key to openness to cultural diversity is to stay curious about why other people behave differently from what we expected.

The second facet of Managing Uncertainty, **Exploring New Approaches**, captures the degree to which we risk trying out new ideas, and welcome cultural differences as a natural and ever-present source of ideas for learning how we could do things differently.

An example of exploring new approaches to doing business comes from a Dutch colleague of ours who moved to Moscow just after the end of the Soviet Union. He was a consultant for one of the big four accounting firms, and he had come to town to do business. Initially he planned his client visits the Dutch way, that is, by agreeing on a date and a time for a first meeting. But this was a tour of frustration – he would arrive on time only to wait for hours or be told that his host was out of the office.

Being a man who is enlivened by difference and risk, he then changed approach. He made a list of potential clients by district and started to drop in without an appointment, asking whether this was a good time to introduce himself and his company's services. If the first potential customer did not have time, he would go to the next, two blocks away, and so on. By arranging his client visits in this new way, he no longer felt frustrated about wasting his time and rushing from one failed appointment to the next, but instead kept relaxed throughout the day and succeeded in having numerous meetings and building up his business.

Another opportunity for exploring new approaches presents itself to many business people who move across the German–Dutch border. Again and again, we have seen that for German business people, this means moving from a rather perfectionist culture, in which they are criticized for the tiniest mistake, to a culture in which people reward quick and improvised solutions because they feel the environment is changing too fast for perfection anyway. How safe will a German engineer feel in following the Dutch approach, and starting to suggest potentially imperfect ideas, at the risk of being remembered as the guy who blundered? And vice versa – how motivated will a Dutch engineer be to learn the code of the more perfectionist culture, accepting the sticklers' obsessive attention to detail and learning to take joy in uncompromisingly creating the ultimate product?

Why is Managing Uncertainty Relevant?

Our culture has taught us how to coordinate our actions with those of others. Letting go of these coordinates, which orient us in what to do when, and what to expect from others, is a call for change – change that may be frightening because we cannot yet feel where it will take us. We may feel as if we are crossing a half-frozen lake in hazy light by jumping from one ice floe to the next, never knowing for sure whether the next floe will hold us, topple over as we touch it or crack smack in the middle.

Uncertainty and how we deal with it has been a topic for many years amongst psychologists. As early as 1971, the developmental psychologist Jerome Kagan argued that all of us have a built-in desire to reduce uncertainty.[31] When we cannot predict what is going to happen, we feel uncertain and want to do something about it. It is like a reflex – in the middle of the deep dark night, we immediately want a flashlight. When we are confronted with two or more conflicting but equally plausible ideas (for instance, 'always tell the truth' and 'show respect to your boss'), or when there is a mismatch between what we thought would happen and what we actually experience (we tell a joke and nobody laughs), we feel uncertain, which motivates us to reduce the uncertainty and get back to where we felt secure. Uncertainty may make us curious, stressed or panicky – but we cannot ignore it.

Our research shows that people who score high on Managing Uncertainty feel more comfortable when interacting with someone from a different cultural background, and are more satisfied with the amount of contact they have with people from a different culture than people who score low on this competence. People who score high on Managing Uncertainty also have more friends from other cultures than people who score low. They are more interested in working abroad and in having work that involves regular cross-cultural interactions, and they are also more confident that they can perform in these work settings than people who score low on Managing Uncertainty.

Some of us have a head start in Managing Uncertainty. The psychologist Richard M. Sorrentino and his colleagues distinguish between people who are uncertainty-oriented and those who are certainty-oriented (see, for instance, their 2008 publication, 'Uncertainty Regulation: The Master Motive'). Uncertainty-oriented people feel at home in uncertain situations: they see such situations as a welcome challenge to clarify what is going on, to dig deeper and analyse discrepancies between what they thought and what they experience. Uncertainty-oriented people have a strong need to know and understand, and uncertain situations fuel this need.[32]

This suggests that when people whom Sorrentino and his team define as uncertainty-oriented move abroad, they are likely to feel comfortable and at ease: there is constant food for thought and action! As a result, they will be curious about the new cultural context and eager to learn more about it, and this will enhance their overall ability to be effective in an intercultural interaction.

Certainty-oriented people, in contrast, may find it hard to accept the uncertainty of cross-cultural interactions because they are constantly out of balance in terms of what they prefer and what they experience. As a result, they may avoid such situations, ignore some of the complications or seek quick fixes to restore certainty. For instance, they will look for what others do, what the experts say or what seems to be commonly accepted wisdom. They not only want a flashlight, but also a map for returning home. In cross-cultural situations, certainty-oriented people may have to work harder to balance their need for certainty with their curiosity about other cultures and their willingness to explore new approaches.

Research by psychologist Lily A. Arasaratnam shows that people's attitude toward uncertainty influences the degree to which they seek intercultural learning opportunities. Arasaratnam argues that some people get a kick out of cross-cultural situations exactly because there is no script for these situations. She suggests that when it comes to intercultural interaction, a personality feature that is often evaluated negatively, namely sensation-seeking, may actually have a lot to offer.[33]

Sensation-seeking is a constant search for novelty and excitement. In today's globalizing world, this may be a great start for becoming interculturally competent. Sensation-seekers seek contact with people from other cultures because these interactions are less certain and predictable than those with people from their own culture – and so offer just the bit of thrill that keeps sensation-seekers awake. If sensation-seekers then use empathy and active listening to truly understand the other person, they have a head start in intercultural competence development compared to those of us who prefer to play it safe.

Exercises

1a) Intercultural Sensitivity, Cultural Awareness: Go to the cinema and watch a film from another culture, in a different language than your own, ideally with a friend or colleague from another culture. Watch and compare your reactions, and how each of you is attempting to make sense of what the characters are doing. Where do your interpretations differ? The different interpretations may give you clues as to how these characters work within their culture. Which themes and motives can you identify that reflect the current situation of the country, or rather appeal to what people from all cultures have tried to come to grips with?

1b) Intercultural Sensitivity, Attention to Signals: Listen to two conversations between strangers (or a friend) and note ten body language signals they give, telling you more than the actual conversation. (For instance, 'Do you think the bus will be here soon?' – do they look at their watch or take out their mobile phone, and does the question arouse anxiety or is it just a casual conversation starter.) Write a short report on what signals you picked up.

2a) Intercultural Communication, Active Listening: There's a joke told by foreigners who move to Ireland and discover the Irish gift for subtext: 'If you say "Good morning" to an Irish person, he may think "Now, what did he mean by that?"' Try to take the same approach to all the conversations you have today – think about the subtext, the subtle inner meanings of everything that is said.

2b) Intercultural Communication, Adapting Communicative Style: Find someone who is from quite a different culture from you – your friend's 17-year-old gamer son; your grandmother's strait-laced bridge partner – and have a conversation with them, taking their cues and adapting your style to suit their way of communicating. Write down what changes you have made in your style of communication – did you lounge and use slang with the gamer, sit up straight and speak precisely with the bridge partner?

3a) Building Commitment, Building Relationships: Look at your most personal relationships, and think about what you do to build mutual commitment. How could you do more – by spending more time together, for instance, or by leaving each other more personal space; by becoming interested in their interests; by surprising them? Mindmap it. Draw a picture of your thoughts.

3b) Building Commitment, Reconciling Stakeholder Needs: Write a short outline of a current dispute you know about. Write the name of each person or group involved at the top of a piece of paper, and list their needs and demands. Describe how you could use commonalities between these people or groups to build bridges and solve their conflicting demands.

4a) Managing Uncertainty, Openness to Cultural Diversity: Test yourself. Find a cinema showing foreign films without subtitles.

Watch three films, trying to follow what is happening between the characters. See whether you enjoy this and find it challenging, or regard it as a crazy waste of time.

4b) Managing Uncertainty, Exploring New Approaches: Go outside and step on the first bus that comes past. Ride it to the terminal and walk for a kilometer or so. Now try to find another bus to get back to your office by asking people in the neighbourhood. Keep track of how the interactions make you feel – are you impatient, do you feel that this is stupid – or are you getting a bang out of the strangeness, and finding that it sparks your creativity?

4

chapter

Different Talents, New Abilities

The four competences of the Intercultural Readiness approach fit together to form an integral picture of a person's strengths, weaknesses, and developmental needs in their ability to deal with other cultures. The competences reflect an idealized sequence of stages in a process of intercultural interaction whereby two or more people from different cultures interact with each other to attain a certain goal.

The process can take five minutes or last for hours, days and months. In its idealized form, the process always involves understanding one another's different perspectives, communicating effectively about these perspectives, finding new solutions to bring these perspectives together and managing the uncertainty that arises from differences between people and the lack of clarity about outcome. These four competences are steps that work together in communicating with people from other cultures, managing multicultural teams and working worldwide.

Cultures Differ, so Do People

People can be very competent in dealing with certain parts of the interaction process, and less skilled with other parts. They can identify their current strengths and weaknesses through assessing their intercultural competences with the Intercultural Readiness Check (IRC), the questionnaire we developed to support people in developing their intercultural readiness. The IRC profile helps people to identify the individual strengths and weaknesses that they bring to the process of intercultural interaction. It indicates which steps they have been mastering well, and which ones they find more difficult.

Many people have a high score on one or two of the four competences, and it is common that people get into the habit of using these talents to compensate for their inability in other areas. For example, someone who is high in Intercultural Communication and Intercultural Sensitivity may not realize – until they have to live and work abroad – that an inability in Managing Uncertainty or Building Commitment is a crippling disadvantage in working daily with people from a different culture.

People who are highly competent in Intercultural Sensitivity may rely too much on this intuitive ability to pick up signals and read situations. People high on the scale in Intercultural Communication may adapt readily to a multiplicity of cultures, but fail to bring their own cultural values and understandings to bear on new situations.

Those who are high in Building Commitment but low on the other competences may rely too much on existing structures, and feel lost when things change. And those skilled in Managing Uncertainty may be open to exploring new ways of doing things, but may not be motivated to reduce their uncertainty by analysing the cultural logics involved in the situation.

What should you do if you score low on a particular competence? And how does this score relate to how well you do with the other competences? A profile produced from the questions answered on the Intercultural Readiness Check can be seen as reflecting an approach that people have already developed. Often, however, this approach can be improved. Feedback on someone's IRC results is the start – and it is possible to learn well and fast by combining the IRC feedback with training and coaching.

With its particular pattern of high and low scores for a person's talent in each individual competence, an IRC profile shows which approach people have already developed. So the goal is to explore how they can improve their approach by using their strengths better, and by developing the weaker competences. They may be relying on existing strengths but be unaware that in doing so, they have been compensating for weaknesses. A good way to look at a profile, then, is to see which strengths they have already developed, and how they can make these even stronger if they also develop the other competences.

High and low scores on the different competences have implications for how people can contribute to the process of intercultural interaction given their current strengths, and what strengths they need to develop. People who score high on Intercultural Sensitivity are good with exploring cultural differences; those with high scores on Intercultural Communication can address differences in appropriate ways. People who are at their best with Building Commitment can creatively draw on different perspectives, developing shared goals, getting people enthusiastic about the solution and following up on it. Those who enjoy Managing Uncertainty can keep up the energy, accept unexpected developments and feel comfortable trying out the new approaches that result from the zingy excitement of the new and strange. How people react to dealing with foreignness – whether this is an Irish person talking to someone from Japan or an artist talking to an academic – varies according to their individual intercultural competences.

Intercultural Sensitivity

Interpreting Low Scores on Intercultural Sensitivity

People scoring low on Intercultural Sensitivity don't have a clear image of the challenge ahead of them. Take the example of the project leader who was sent with his team to Thailand to negotiate with a local company on the construction of a golf course and associated accommodation facilities. They had one week before they had to return home. Their Thai counterparts were very friendly and welcoming and insisted on taking the team around. One social event followed another, the team met many 'top' people, but none of them seemed willing to get down to real business. On the day of departure, frustrated, the project leader concluded that his team had not made any progress.

With lack of Intercultural Sensitivity, this project leader only approached the week in terms of what he would have liked to get out of it – to get down to business. He was not prepared to perceive the meeting as an opportunity to get to know each other well, and to build effective relationships which would make doing business easier later on.

Instead of thoroughly understanding different perspectives involved, people who have not developed Intercultural Sensitivity assume too many similarities; think that superficial adaptation is enough, without trying to really understand where their counterpart is coming from. They are easily satisfied with what they know rather than trying to find a new interpretation of the situation. People with this approach to cultural differences may find it difficult to respect other cultures whilst at the same time staying true to themselves. And they may underestimate how much others may have already adapted to them in the joint effort of creating common ground.

They may not invest enough time in finding multiple interpretations of a situation, and may evaluate situations too quickly. Since their scope is limited, they lack a frame of reference within which they could clarify different interpretations, perspectives, intentions and expectations.

Low on Intercultural Sensitivity, High on the Other Competences

People who score low on Intercultural Sensitivity will use their other competences, always within a limited understanding of the situation – an understanding that is mainly influenced by their own norms and values – to try and find solutions from within their frame of reference. If they score high on the other three competences, then they may convince others of their perspective, in a way that doesn't offend and may even be motivating. But they themselves will miss out on the learning experience that comes with exploring culturally different perspectives.

A surprising finding from the IRC database is that people may score just below average even though they have spent considerable time abroad. This may indicate that they see interpersonal and intercultural effectiveness predominantly in terms of getting along with people, and any focus on differences feels to them like being unkind and creating distance. With the best of intentions, they shy away from exploring different perspectives. The unfortunate result of this may be that they rely too much on their own cultural perspective. The people they meet see the good intentions and are relieved that contact has been established in good faith, and the person succeeds again and again at forming relationships. While they succeed in establishing relationships, their lack of Intercultural Sensitivity will keep them from exploring cultural differences more deeply, and discovering how understanding these differences deepens understanding of others and ourselves.

DEVELOPING INTERCULTURAL SENSITIVITY

If you believe you would score rather low on Intercultural Sensitivity, here are some tips on what you could do:

- Learn more about your own cultural background(s). How did your culture's values develop over time? Which events shaped its history? What do people from other cultures say about your culture(s)?

- Learn more about a culture that is relevant to you – through workshop materials, movies, literature, conversations with colleagues and so on.

- Try to suspend judgement, for instance, by comparing your interpretation of your actions and events with those of someone you know well but who tends to have different opinions.

- Do you sense a hidden message? Think about what people might find comfortable stating in public, and which subjects they would rather address informally or through third parties.

Pay attention to the relationships between people in a public setting.

- People communicate indirectly to avoid loss of face – learn to read between the lines, in particular in face-threatening situations involving giving feedback and giving instructions.

- Do the nonverbal signals support what is said, or is there a mismatch?

- Culture reference guides, foreign movies and novels provide valuable information about how people use verbal and nonverbal signals.

- Cultures differ in how and when emotions are shown in public. How can you become more comfortable with people who express their emotions more strongly, or less strongly than you?

Interpreting High Scores on Intercultural Sensitivity

People who have Intercultural Sensitivity as a high score may be very capable of mapping the different cultural perspectives in a *conceptual* way, skilled in weighing the pros and cons, and estimating the complexity of a situation. They may be good at continually generating new interpretations, and seeing their own point of view as one among others, rather than the only right one. High scorers on Intercultural Sensitivity are good at describing a situation, creating more than one interpretation and being cautious with judging. If they score low on the other dimensions, this can be because they are rather introverted, and excel at a cognitive, intellectual approach to the field.

People with such a competence profile can contribute to the intercultural process by anticipating potential problems, and so may contribute greatly in the beginning, where we need to chart our differences. They may be perceivers, introverted thinkers. In negotiations, they may be very good in the first phase, where the parties need to identify the gap between their offers.

High on Intercultural Sensitivity, Low on the Other Competences

What about people who score high on Intercultural Sensitivity but low on the other IRC competences? What workarounds are they likely to use? People with such a competence profile may tend to fall back on their Intercultural Sensitivity – and do so even more when there is a lot of pressure (Answer the questions in Figure 4.1 to test your Intercultural Sensitivity.). They will focus mainly on getting a clear idea of the cultural differences at play, looking for more and more nuances and sensitivities. They may worry that talking about the differences may be too confrontational, and may

Intercultural Sensitivity is the degree to which we take an active interest in others, their cultural background, needs and perspectives.

How do you see yourself? Please tick three strengths and three potential pitfalls that you feel apply to you.

Cultural Awareness

Strengths	Potential Pitfalls
I'm aware of my own cultural values and able to articulate them	I haven't thought about how my opinions are influenced by my cultural background
I recognize that my own judgements and opinions are influenced by my cultural background	I do not differentiate much between cultural differences encountered so far
	I am not interested in other cultural norms and values
I can describe different cultural perspectives, such as different approaches to time, status, groups and the importance of relationships	I base my decisions largely on my own cultural understanding of situations

Attention to Signals

Strengths	Potential Pitfalls
I'm sensitive to issues of status, politeness and face in communication	I only adapt to local culture on a superficial level, but don't go deeper
I'm aware of different (non)verbal signals (for instance, silences in Asia)	I tend to overlook nonverbal signals
I check that others understand my meaning	I assume people have understood and agreed
I listen actively and carefully	I don't double check

FIG 4.1 Intercultural Sensitivity self-check

fear to give offence by challenging others to acknowledge the difference and start creating a shared approach.

People scoring high only on Intercultural Sensitivity may tend to seek energy and calm in themselves, by trying to develop a frame of reference that allows them to pinpoint the areas of the biggest cultural differences. With this strategy working really well, they may see no need to envision how else they could contribute to the process and strengthen other competences. Their strength is therefore limited in range, because they may find it difficult to engage whenever the cross-cultural dialogue gets complex and develops its own dynamic; they may not then be able to swiftly adapt to that dynamic.

People who are high on Intercultural Sensitivity but low on Building Commitment may find it difficult to go beyond the frames of reference that they so clearly see, by developing a new shared element. If they score low on Managing Uncertainty, they may find it difficult to tolerate the uncertainty of intercultural settings over a long time, and quickly feel drained. For example, if English is not their native language, they may, towards the end of a business meeting held in English, lean over to their colleague and start a side conversation in their native language. When this happens, it is clearly time to take a break.

Intercultural Communication

Interpreting Low Scores on Intercultural Communication

Intercultural Communication scores reflect the degree to which people actively monitor how they communicate. People who score low on Intercultural Communication may tend to focus mainly on the meaning they want to get across, rather than on the needs and expectations of their listeners (see Box 4.1 for some examples). They are not sufficiently mindful when communicating with others, and don't sufficiently adjust how they communicate in line with cultural requirements.

BOX 4.1 MARKETING ACROSS CULTURES

A failing in the Intercultural Communication skill led to a tragic fiasco for a company that made an indigestion remedy – if the urban legend is true. Their advertisement was a cartoon strip with no words. On the left-hand side was a man clutching his stomach in pain; in the next scene, he drank down their remedy, and in the final scene, he was beaming and happy.

The company had forgotten that in Arab countries, people read from right to left, and the marketers were puzzled when, sadly, sales failed to take off in the Middle East.

Similarly, a western company used to selling large bottles of detergent at a cheap rate – 'buy two gallons for the price of one' style – found that consumers in India were instead buying its competitors' more expensive detergents in smaller amounts. It took local knowledge to sort out the problem: people simply could not budget for the large bottles. The company changed its strategy to sell small amounts cheaply, and sales took off.

People who score low on Intercultural Communication tend to be impatient when interacting with others, believing that things will run more smoothly if they exert more pressure. They may interrupt others without checking whether this fits their pace and style; come across as tense and unbending, and express attention and interest in a topic (through tone of voice, eye contact, body language, and so on) in ways that listeners from other cultures misinterpret. As a result of these mutual misinterpretations, they may end up being perceived as brash and angry – or as withholding, shy and unassertive.

People with these low scores on Intercultural Communication may need to learn to manage turn-taking in ways that match their listeners' expectations (eye contact, speed, pausing, intonation), especially in formal situations and in group discussions, where people may be using different turn-taking rules. They may not know how and when to take their turn to speak, and when to stop and give the listener a turn. They may express their emotions in ways that are appropriate in their own culture but confusing to people from other cultural backgrounds, who may have learned either to subdue the same emotions or to express them more strongly.

DEVELOPING INTERCULTURAL COMMUNICATION

If you believe you would score rather low on Intercultural Communication, here are some tips on what you could do:

- When working with people from other cultures, deliberately take more time before responding than you would otherwise.

- Rephrase other people's statements neutrally before commenting on them.

- Prepare for difficult situations like giving feedback and raising sensitive topics. Do you need to address the issue immediately, or should you wait for a better moment?

- When you need to criticize, ensure that you have developed the proper relational context that will allow you to give feedback constructively.

- Find out how verbal and nonverbal signals are used in one or more cultures that are relevant to you – through culture-specific books, language training or conversations with colleagues. Consider watching foreign movies together with cultural insiders, who can share their interpretations with you.

- Gestures may differ in meaning across cultures. If you are uncertain about what a gesture means, don't use it. (For instance, the finger-and-thumb-in-a-circle that means 'A-OK' to Americans is close to a sign meaning something very rude in Brazil.)

- Be careful with showing negative emotions like anger, irritation and exasperation. Wait until people know you better and have a broader basis for judging how strongly you really feel about an issue.

Interpreting High Scores on Intercultural Communication

People who score high on Intercultural Communication adapt and listen well. They can quickly sense that the people around them may have other needs than they expected at first, even if they do not know much about the others' cultural background, or did not reflect much ahead of time about the different perspectives that may play a role in the situation. They have a well-developed radar for what is appropriate to address in a given situation, because they are alert and tuned-in, and listen to what people say, and what they don't say. They can often create a good atmosphere that makes it easier for the others to share a lot of information, and will be good at working on the spot with the information they are receiving.

A person who scores high on Intercultural Communication can greatly contribute to the four steps of the intercultural process by helping people connect to each other, and by addressing in sensitive ways the different views and expectations that are being revealed as people are communicating with each other.

High on Intercultural Communication, Low on Other Intercultural Competences

An example of someone who uses an extraordinary level of skill in Inter-cultural Communication to compensate for lower skills in others is, according to our remote analysis, the Dutch soccer genius Johan Cruyff (Box 4.2).

BOX 4.2 EL CANT DEL BARÇA[1]

Cruyff's great skill as a player was his vision of the overall structure and tactics of a game he was playing in; he seemed to be everywhere on the field, making play, scoring, defusing the opposing team's carefully-built strategy.

As a manager he brought his skill in communication to bear – as demonstrated by the pure cultural loyalty of calling his newborn son Jordi in 1974 after Barcelona's first win against rival Madrid – Jordi is the proud name of a Catalan hero, and this name was forbidden to Catalonians for many years by Generalísimo Franco, who had crushed Catalonian independence and centred his rule in the rival Madrid.

When Cruyff became manager at Barcelona, he introduced a style known as 'tiki-taka', with fast passing and working the ball through various channels to keep possession. He was a hugely successful manager, beloved by fans and players, but perhaps a little less so by the management team because of his mercurial temperament.

He left amid conflict with the management; a couple of years later, in December 1999, a tribute match was held, pitting Cruyff's Barcelona 'Dream Team' of the early 1990s against the 1999 Barcelona team.

The stadium was packed with almost 100,000 spectators, including world star, Eric Cantona, and at the end of the game the crowd exploded in cheers as Cruyff walked to the centre of the Camp Nou pitch, at the hub of a wheel of players who circled him again and again, running to the resounding roar of Catalans.

At last, Cruyff held up his hand to make the usual tactful thanks-to-everyone farewell speech. But as the management that had let him go sat with stiff smiles, he made the speech they didn't expect.

This was not the time to address any problems, said Cruyff – and then he called for the singing of the club anthem. As the crowd roared out *El Cant Del Barça*, the club song that symbolized their Catalan pride, the management had to sit there, applauding: a prime example of using Intercultural Communication; less so of Building Commitment!

As with the other three competences, the risk for people scoring high on Intercultural Communication but clearly *lower* on the other competences is that they may overly rely on their communicative agility. They will miss important opportunities to get the extra value out of cultural diversity because they do not dig deeper, don't challenge perspectives and don't envision as the ultimate goal a solution in which both or more perspectives are reconciled in a new approach.

People scoring high on Intercultural Communication may then place too much trust in their skill in responding flexibly to unexpected demands, seeing this as the secret formula for being interculturally effective. But they only understand success in intercultural relationships in terms of being able to adapt to the demands of the current situation. The downside of their approach is that they may adapt to what the majority wants or what the last person just said, without working out the differences and integrating them in a shared perspective.

Someone who is strong in Intercultural Communication but weaker in one or more of the other three competences may need to work on a more thorough understanding of the various perspectives in a situation. Such perspectives, which may be revealed only *partly* during a particular interaction, may have important implications that show up in other situations, when contracts need to be drawn.

Our culture is like the water fish swim in – we don't need to think much about it. So in a real situation we may find it difficult to explain our views, needs and obligations in sufficient detail for someone from another culture, who may understand things quite differently. In consequence, just relying on the information gained during a smoothly managed conversation is risky – a lot may not be revealed. By shying away from a deeper understanding of their own and others' perspectives, people scoring high on Intercultural Communication and low on other competences may fail to use their skills to explain their own perspective, and to help others explain *their* perspective.

People who score high on Intercultural Communication and low on the other three competences lack a thorough understanding of the value differences that come into play in any intercultural relationship. They miss a well-developed frame of reference for addressing all pros and cons, all ifs and buts, and potentially conflicting future consequences of the perspectives at issue. In a negotiation, for example, despite their flexibility they may leave the other party in a negotiation feeling a little betrayed. Great communicators can be great intercultural communicators only if they hone their other intercultural competences as well. (See Figure 4.2 to test your level of Intercultural Communication.)

The degree to which we actively monitor how we communicate.

How do you see yourself? Please tick three strengths and three potential pitfalls.

Active Listening

Strengths	Potential Pitfalls
I'm aware of different communication styles	I tend to ignore the perspective of others
I listen and observe well	I get frustrated
I'm aware of different preferences for hinting and directness	I tend to criticize other people's way of doing things
I'm sensitive to issues of status and face, and how this influences what is said and not said	I can be insensitive in how and when I bring across negative messages

Adjusting Communicative Style

Strengths	Potential Pitfalls
I modify my own degree of directness when giving instructions or feedback	I interrupt often, or remain too silent
I take care when criticizing others or giving bad news	I use a mono-style; I don't adapt (for instance, 'I always start with a good joke')
I modulate my pace and volume when speaking, and pause to match others' pace and volume	I repeat points to push them. I'm biased, careless in rephrasing other people's statements
I seek clarification	I don't adapt my level of directness to requirements of status, politeness and face (for instance, 'I'm always upfront with them, and at the end of the day, they respect me for that')
I encourage participation, I'm interested	

FIG 4.2 Intercultural Communication self-check

Building Commitment

Interpreting Low Scores on Building Commitment

If people score low on the key cultural competence of Building Commitment, they will find it hard to go beyond seemingly opposite value orientations. They don't see how they can adapt to the other culture and still arrive at a solution that works in both cultural frameworks – the other party's and their own. They may overly push for their own approach, regardless of the culture in which it is supposed to be implemented, or they may throw their own approach overboard because they do not see how it could possibly fit with what they take to be the local norms.

We once heard a speaker discard the company's approach he had just been advocating based on a superficial understanding of different local practices. His approach reflected that of someone scoring low on Building Commitment. The speaker explained to his audience the code of conduct of a western company. He went into great detail about how all gift-giving practices were seen as undesirable and unacceptable by his company. After the presentation a US American working in Indonesia commented, 'In Indonesia, I am in a very different context. In Indonesia, gift-giving is an essential and widely accepted part of building a business relationships. What should I do?' To which the speaker replied, 'Well, Indonesia is different. You have to work out your own solution. Basically, in Indonesia, you're on your own.'

People scoring low on Building Commitment find it hard to create a complex frame of reference through which different cultural viewpoints and needs would be integrated in a larger picture. In a cross-cultural conflict, of which the code of conduct around giving and receiving gifts is an example, they may only be concerned about gifts reflecting attempts at bribery. They may fail to conceive of the possibility that their business partners work with clear codes about which gifts are appropriate to build a business relationship, which gifts would oblige them to return favours they don't want to return, and which ones would be clear instances of bribery, and so forbidden.

People scoring low on Building Commitment are likely to try to resolve value conflicts like this by pushing their own views, or to resort to doing nothing other than adapt to the others in the interaction, or to seek compromise as their ultimate goal. These conflict management styles all have their place and time, but in a cross-cultural context, they fail to create commitment from all parties in the long run.

A compromise is often mistaken for a reconciled solution, but the difference is clear: reconciled solutions give energy, and so can be immediately recognized and distinguished from compromise, which are mostly a little draining. By definition, a compromise means that each party has to give a little (or a lot) in order to get a little (or a lot). Compromise means that people need to stay in control mode. Because the compromise solution does not inspire people, their intrinsic motivation to implement this solution is not guaranteed. But people who stay in control mode miss the chance to discover that they can trust the other party.

A reconciled solution – a solution that fully meets the needs of both parties involved – is different, and, importantly, it builds trust. Trust reduces the need for constant monitoring, freeing everybody to do better things. In a cross-cultural context, it is of particular importance that parties agree on an approach through which they can learn to trust each other, so that they in turn can more easily develop and implement successful solutions, and continue to build trust between each other.

Low on Building Commitment, High on Other Intercultural Competences

If people score *high* on *other* intercultural competences but low on Building Commitment, they can analyse the different frames of reference, and can also move in between them, learning more about different frames through skilled conversations in which they signal empathy and understanding. But they are not able to derive from this a shared new solution to a nagging and complex issue (see Box 4.3 for a familiar example). Because their solutions only work for some time, and for some parties, their network will stay relatively small, consisting of patches of islands that are not connected.

BOX 4.3 LOW ON BUILDING COMMITMENT, HIGH ON OTHER COMPETENCES

A classic example of someone who is low on Building Commitment but high in the other three competences of Intercultural Sensitivity, Intercultural Communication and

> Managing Uncertainty is the marriage counsellor in that old anecdote, who listens first to a wife explaining all the things that are wrong with her husband and wrecking their marriage. 'You're completely right,' says the counsellor.
>
> Then he listens to the husband, who recites a long litany of complaints about his wife. 'You're completely right,' the counsellor tells him.
>
> The lawyer who has been sitting with the counsellor while this is going on is puzzled, and asks, 'Surely they can't both be right?'
>
> The counsellor admits that this is so, and tells the lawyer, 'You're completely right.'

People who score low on Building Commitment but are highly competent in Managing Uncertainty, Intercultural Sensitivity and Intercultural Communication can become stuck in 'analysis paralysis' when they have to work with groups from several countries.

Today's call for corporate social responsibility is a case in point, one example being corporations that sell technology or clothing to well-off consumers in the wealthy west, but have this manufactured in developing countries. Scandals involving exploitation of teenage workers, suicides, factory accidents and related problems must be addressed, even if the corporations do this only because the scandals shock public opinion and make customers back off from their brands.

Corporate executives need to really know how to build commitment, since they must resolve the interests of at least three stakeholders – the working people who make their goods, the customers who buy them and their company. In practice, this requires building commitment with many stakeholders, including factory owners, the people working for them, unions, staff, competitors who are using the same facilities or operate in the same country, and also government agencies and NGOs like the Clean Clothes Campaign, which rightly keep pushing corporations to do more.

Some companies have been proactive in building commitment through ethical policies; for instance, PVH Corp, whose brands include Calvin Klein and Tommy Hilfiger, and Tchibo, which uses its established coffee brand Tchibo to sell coffee and a broad range of non-food products, were the first to sign the legally binding Accord on Fire and Building Safety. The clothing giants Hennes & Mauritz (H&M) and Inditex, with brands including Zara and Massimo Dutti, also decided to sign the agreement.

Developments like these show that building commitment may also mean joining powers, and using power. Apart from their intrinsic interest in doing the right thing, these companies are keenly aware that their customers care about the way in which their clothes and high tech products are produced, and that companies can only ensure a strong brand image in the long run if they can convince consumers that they have been building commitment with key stakeholders in the entire supply chain.

Because Building Commitment stands out in the IRC database as the competence that is more commonly developed among senior executives than among less senior managers, a low score in this competence is a particular handicap for those who have or seek responsibility for global leadership.

People who score low on this vital competence will often have invented a series of compromise solutions, but this means they have to stay in control mode. They may travel constantly across the globe to their company's various locations to ensure that everybody still sticks to the agreement. They can miss their chance to move up in the organization because they are too often on a plane instead of building their networks both at headquarters and in their company's various locations.

DEVELOPING BUILDING COMMITMENT

If you believe you would score rather low on Building Commitment, here are some tips on what you could do:

- How important are networks for your work? If you need them, ensure that you establish and maintain such networks across cultures.

- Think of interesting topics and try to find like-minded people. Keep in mind that one usually needs to invest time in any network before benefiting from it.

- Are there interesting topics on which networks are based that open tremendous opportunities for networking?

- Find key local contacts that can advise you and introduce you to the right people.

- Think of formal and informal occasions for bringing people together and encouraging exchanges between them.

- Pay attention to the personal aspects of a work relationship. It does not mean you have to become personal friends with all your colleagues. It just means acknowledging that the quality of relationships influences the quality of work.

- Acknowledge that individuals differ in their viewpoints and priorities. Learn about their perspectives, aspirations and challenges so that you can take into account their concerns when recommending steps later on.

- Study people's objections to your approach. Look for what is constructive in what they are saying. Try and see resistance as an opportunity to learn.

- Envisage the potential objections of key stakeholders so that you can address their concerns when recommending solutions.

- When faced with a problem or conflict, show that you are interested and concerned; make sure to ask questions before suggesting solutions.

- When working in a multicultural team, take extra time to ensure that you understand everyone's work preferences and obligations. Expect more misunderstandings than in monocultural teams, and take time to clarify these.

Interpreting High Scores on Building Commitment

People who score high on Building Commitment have a knack for letting their networks grow through the power of their reconciled solutions. Reconciled solutions give energy. They are therefore low-maintenance solutions, freeing all parties to focus on more important things than mutual checks and controls. Reconciled solutions don't just solve a problem – they integrate people and give them a shared sense of direction. Therefore, reconciled solutions get people intrinsically motivated to implement them. With all people aligned behind the solution and committed to implementing, and in so doing using all their culture-specific insider's knowledge, people can be at their best. As a result, they learn to trust each other, both emotionally and competence-wise, and there is less and less need for costly controls.

Local values can be universal, like the Texan advice 'never slap a man chewing tobacco'. They can also be deeply held and deeply different. An example of this is the strong value of competition in some western societies, compared with the equally strongly-held value of cooperation in other societies.

International companies rooted in a competition culture may find it difficult to motivate staff from a cooperation culture. A solution has been found in the concept of 'coopetition', where, for instance, rather than giving a bonus to the highest-performing salesman or saleswoman, instead the highest performers are invited to give motivating speeches to their teams on what they have learned, and the individual who is most successful in sharing his or her learning receives an award that is shared with the team.

A person who scores high on Building Commitment can greatly contribute to the process of intercultural interaction by drawing together all the input from the different parties, reflecting on them and proposing a solution that integrates everyone's visions and views. This will be a turning point in the development of their intercultural interaction, since everybody sees that their own input, and their own efforts to contribute, based on their intercultural competences, have been honoured and have made a difference.

High on Building Commitment, Low on Other Intercultural Competences

If a person *only* scores high on Building Commitment, but not on the other competences, then this talent, which has the potential to be so powerful, loses power. People like this tend to rely too much on the networks that others built before them, as for example in embassies where local codes of conduct and ways of dealing with issues have been developed long before the new ambassador moves in.

Building Commitment is almost a universal competence among diplomats, who may, however, be surprisingly lacking in Intercultural Sensitivity, Intercultural Communication and Managing Uncertainty. A common workaround is seen in the international diplomatic code, where a separate, international culture has been built for diplomats. They host their colleagues from other embassies at events celebrating their national anniversaries and their artistic, literary and business icons, they invite other envoys to state visits. There is a whole ritual with its own expectations and rules that involves the diplomatic services of all countries, connecting them in another dimension and side-lining the fact that they come from different cultures.

Another example of this workaround is companies with a strong brand and a multinational presence – a company like Disney, which sells dolls and toys modelled on its cartoon characters, may actively avoid localizing them. You don't see Mickey Mouse with a little moustache and a baguette in Disneyland Paris. Mickey Mouse, like Superman, Totoro and the DeLorean car in *Back to the Future*, transcends national cultures and belongs to his own supranational culture.

This is a workaround that can be used by those who seek to transcend local differences and unite staff from many cultures: form a brand that is almost a nation unto itself, through which staff, and even customers, can relate to each other.

Such well-designed networks may also exist in a business, with routine meetings for bringing people together and having them share information, using jargon, slang and jokes only the insiders understand. The approach has its disadvantages: with the same people meeting each other all the time, there is not much fresh input or information on potential developments – no need is seen for investing in dialogue with strangers who may help to challenge and expand old frames of reference.

People who have focused only on developing their talent for Building Commitment may rely too much on networks like this, with their familiar ways of dealing with difference. They grew into these networks, focused their energy on understanding the networks and getting in. These networks are the measure of their success. People who only focus on Building Commitment have not paid enough attention to other ways of measuring success or complementing their idea of what success means.

People who rely on the old networks and old ways do not get energy from intercultural interactions – they are not interested enough in where new people are coming from, and they fail to develop the skill of bridging cultural differences through adaptive communication. People who score high on Building Commitment but low on the other three IRC competences can be highly effective managers in their *own* culture, where they have learned to balance the dilemma between task focus and relationship management. But they may not yet have tried to transfer that ability to a culturally more demanding context.

People who score high both on Building Commitment and the other competences see to it that they constantly get new input. But those who *only* score high on Building Commitment do not search for new information to feed into their system. Their strength is to create an atmosphere of calmness and balance. But if they are satisfied with this, and their Building Commitment remains an isolated strength, this limits them. Their networks may become obsolete over time, since they lack fresh input and so only generate solutions with people who less and less reflect today's and tomorrow's reality.

There is another danger: while high scores on Building Commitment may make someone a very successful manager in his or her own culture, it is exactly this aura of success that turns into a shield that can be used against conflicting and challenging input coming from people who have developed other IRC competences and so try and bring new input and viewpoints. (See Figure 4.3 for a Building Commitment self-check.)

Building commitment captures the degree to which we actively try to influence our social environment, based on a concern for relationships and integrating people.

How do you see yourself? Please tick three strengths and three potential pitfalls.

Building Relationships

Strengths	Potential Pitfalls
I stimulate exchange and collaboration between people	I don't invest much in relationships across cultures
I develop relationships that allow me to give constructive feedback	I do not find out about the different work preferences of the people I work with
I develop relationships to encourage motivation and commitment from people	I don't seek contact outside my cultural group
I use internal and external networks for advice and consultation	I do not develop appropriate relational context to manage people effectively
	I do not communicate concerns to others

Reconciling Stakeholder Needs

Strengths	Potential Pitfalls
I weigh many different angles and opinions on a problem in order to solve it	I try to impose my expectations, for instance, around timeframes and deadlines
I am not satisfied with simple compromise	When faced with cross-cultural dilemma, I tend to avoid or sidestep it
I come up with flexible solutions that integrate others' beliefs and preferences	I ignore different perspectives when looking for solutions
I consider long-term implications of decisions	I tend to offer compromise

---

FIG 4.3   **Building Commitment self-check**

Managing Uncertainty

Interpreting Low Scores on Managing Uncertainty

A *low* score on **Managing Uncertainty** indicates someone who will quickly run out of energy and become tired of the effort of interacting with people from other cultures. This is so even for people who are good with all the other steps in the process of interaction. In the good moments, they do all the right things, but even then intercultural interaction remains emotional and challenging at some perhaps as yet ill-understood level of psychological functioning.

International students, for example, may have an optimistic self-image, regarding themselves as good at dealing with cultural diversity, because they have travelled the world and visited many places. However if they lack the important competence of Managing Uncertainty, when they are posted abroad and have to live in a new culture, this self-image may change dramatically. Now, rather than being foreign consumers of interesting quaintness, they have to live within the culture and accept the challenge of its norms – a totally different experience that challenges their ability to relax into the new and strange.

If you have a low score on Managing Uncertainty, but you score well on Intercultural Sensitivity, Intercultural Communication and Building Commitment, the factor you need to manage is yourself. For example, 'When I go to Thailand on business,' says a partner in a multinational agency, 'I do all the things that will contribute to the success of my assignment in predictable ways. I stay in a Hilton hotel, I order a limousine to bring me there from the airport rather than having the stress of explaining my destination to a taxi driver, and I eat a western meal in the hotel.

All these things are normal and predictable for me, and do not tap into my energy resources.

So when the moment comes when I am sitting in front of the Thai negotiators, I have energy left to deal with the interaction. I am not exhausted by navigating a strange hotel, dealing with new food or trying to talk to a taxi driver using a Thai language handbook. Later, when the negotiation is over, I can enjoy taking local taxis, eating Thai food, just being in Bangkok.'

For people who score low on Managing Uncertainty, those intercultural interactions are not a good place to recharge the batteries. Instead, their batteries are recharged when they are back with people they know well, where they can relax and let go, not worrying about doing the right thing and being accepted. They haven't yet learned to seek energy through the new relations they have built, the goodwill, the shared understanding with those who are different. They may be aware of the uncertainty, but it does not help them revitalize themselves. And they may find it particularly difficult to develop this competence if their environment constantly rewards them for avoiding uncertainty (see Box 4.4 for an example).

BOX 4.4 ORGANIZATIONAL ENVIRONMENT AND INDIVIDUAL MANAGING UNCERTAINTY COMPETENCE

Dutch and German organizations tend to function very differently in how they deal with uncertainty: German organizations invest much more attention and energy into avoiding uncertainty than Dutch ones. This difference can lead to frictions and conflict in German–Dutch collaborations, regardless of how much the people involved like each other. German organizations and their people are usually very open towards, and interested in, the Dutch culture; they admire it in many ways and are curious about it. Germans tend to like the Dutch, appreciating them for being informal, relaxed, friendly and not so hierarchical. (This is a common pattern between neighbouring countries differing in size: people of the larger country like the people from the smaller country, whereas the people from the smaller country respect the bigger country for its competences but don't automatically like the country.[2])

When it comes to planning their joint work, however, both the Dutch and the German parties see how their different organizational work practices create issues for the other. Dutch people are typically more at ease with improvisation, not fixing agreements to the last comma, trusting each other to do their best on the spot. Fixing all agreements in writing suffocates them; they feel constrained and patronized. They work hard towards consensus, making sure everybody understands the big picture and the overall guidelines. We have heard a Dutch CEO call the idea of voting for a decision a practice that treats people like *stemvee* ('voting cattle').

Their German counterparts can get nervous with this approach, certainly if they discover that what was written down after a meeting was interpreted only as a summary of the discussion, whereas they took it to be the decisions reached. With all this openness to future action, how can they possibly anticipate difficulties, prevent mistakes and avoid making a fool of themselves? They must spell out the details and agree on them in writing! It just feels better.

If a German member of a Dutch–German integration team scores low on Managing Uncertainty, he or she may find it especially difficult to deal with the greater degrees of freedom the Dutch feel so comfortable with – regardless of how well they connect to their Dutch colleagues and enjoy working with them. They will find it exhausting to leave things open, constantly envisioning worst-case scenarios that they should have predicted and prevented. At the very least, to them, the Dutch open approach to planning presents an unnecessary complication of a smooth-running workflow.

An example of a problem caused by a low score on Managing Uncertainty is a German firm that negotiated with Dutch colleagues on a collaboration. A meeting was held, and it was agreed to use a specific high-quality and low-price supplier.

Some weeks later the Germans discovered that, without consulting them, the Dutch had used a different supplier. They were furious; the Dutch were puzzled. 'Yeah, but after the meeting we discovered another supplier, even cheaper and better quality, so why would we implement the stupid decision of the meeting?' they asked tactfully.

The Germans exploded. 'This is sabotage! If you wanted to change the outcome, go to the supplier we've chosen together and push for a better price and quality.' Mutual bafflement ensued.

DEVELOPING MANAGING UNCERTAINTY

If you believe you would score rather low on Managing Uncertainty, here are some tips on what you could do:

- Find out more about your own culture and how it has influenced you. Which values did your parents try to instil in you, which behaviour was rewarded at school? And how did this early cultural training help you to anticipate which behaviour would be rewarded at work?

- When going on holiday, which country do you enjoy most? Find out more about this country.

- Find out more about a person from another culture whom you deeply respect or admire. What unique challenges have they faced in their environment? How did they overcome those challenges?

- Think back to when you successfully adapted to a new situation (say, starting your professional training, working for a new company). What did you do to adapt and how could this help you to approach unknown situations now?

- If you are not immediately excited about a new approach, imagine practising it as long as you wish to with no one watching you. How long do you need to feel comfortable with the new approach? Add one month on top of it, and then picture yourself wholly enjoying its benefits and feeling good about yourself.

- Try to balance new experiences with familiar ones. Working with people from different cultures can be stressful. Make sure you combine the challenge with activities you find enjoyable and reassuring.

- Imagine an intercultural situation – for instance, an outdoor event for a team of Jamaican, Irish and Nigerian managers in the Algerian desert – and see how you would run it. Would you be satisfied only with perfection? What would happen if things did not run perfectly smoothly?

Interpreting High Scores on Managing Uncertainty

People scoring high on Managing Uncertainty will seek the uncertainty, and thrive on it; they will get energy from people who are different from them, because the differences challenge and motivate them.

We have worked with a German manager who was the director of a Belgian company, just having returned from 12 years in Sao Paulo. She had top scores on Managing Uncertainty and thoroughly enjoyed the excitement of a reorganization she had just initiated. Within two years, the organization had doubled the turnover with the same number of people, and all members of the management team had grown both professionally and personally through a long-term management development programme that accompanied the reorganization.

People scoring high on Managing Uncertainty can contribute to the intercultural process because they are good at keeping everyone alert and motivated to deal with the vagaries and uncertainties until solutions are clear and a plan for implementation is on the table. They don't seek shortcuts to reducing certainty, like pushing for their own approach, or the one that is most convenient, seeking a quick fix. Nor will they allow people to retreat into their safe harbour of their own cultural group. People scoring high on Managing Uncertainty can be an invaluable asset in culturally diverse teams because they do not seek safety and relief in cuddling up in their cultural in-group within their team.

High on Managing Uncertainty, Low on the Other Competences

People scoring high on Managing Uncertainty but *low* on the other competences may risk keeping others at bay because they are not really interested in them as individuals, as people. They like working across cultures for the cognitive challenge this brings. They may overestimate the degree to which others enjoy the challenge as much as they do – when in fact others may need more psychological safety, structure, predictability, the comfort of similarity, cohesion and harmony in the team. If their team or organization is going through an emotionally taxing time, for example a reorganization or a merger, people scoring high on Managing Uncertainty but low on the other intercultural competences may not be emotionally close enough to the people around them, and so may not sense how much others feel threatened. As a result, they may miss out on moments where they should reassure their colleagues and help them to find a new balance, so that the colleagues, too, start feeling safe and secure again because they feel they're understood. (Use Figure 4.3 to assess your abilities in Managing Uncertainty; then review all your self-checks from the chapter in Box 4.5 and find out how you can enhance your intercultural effectiveness in Box 4.6.)

Managing Uncertainty captures the degree to which we see the uncertainty and complexity of culturally diverse environments as an opportunity for personal development.

How do you see yourself? Please tick three strengths and three potential pitfalls.

Openness to Cultural Diversity

Strengths	Potential Pitfalls
I feel comfortable with uncertain and ambiguous situations	I feel most comfortable in clear and predictable situations
I'm ready to face the added complexity of international assignments or work relations	I shy away from intercultural interactions because they do not give me the sense of certainty that I experience as pleasant
I'm curious to know more about other people's cultural background	I feel threatened by 'informational overload' or by events that I can't readily explain
I'm interested in working in other cultures	

Exploring New Approaches

Strengths	Potential Pitfalls
I enjoy trying out new things, improvising, taking risks	I stick to my own approach rather than try out something new
I like experiencing new activities	I see different ways of behaving, but I don't try them out
I seek new ways of doing things	I need time to adjust to new practices
I integrate new data and experiences into my own way of doing things	I use a single approach when trying to solve problems or work with people

FIG 4.4   **Managing Uncertainty self-check**

BOX 4.5 REVIEW YOUR SELF-CHECKS

Intercultural Sensitivity

Your three strengths: Your three potential pitfalls:
1   1
2   2
3   3

Intercultural Communication

Your three strengths: Your three potential pitfalls:
1   1
2   2
3   3

Building Commitment

Your three strengths: Your three potential pitfalls:
1   1
2   2
3   3

Managing Uncertainty

Your three strengths: Your three potential pitfalls:
1   1
2   2
3   3

BOX 4.6 ENHANCING YOUR INTERCULTURAL EFFECTIVENESS

What is most important to you right now:

- to connect better to other people,

- to perform more effectively in your intercultural work, or

- to enjoy your intercultural interactions more than you do now?

Depending on your goals:

- Which of the strengths you've identified helps you to achieve your goals?

- Which pitfalls could you start addressing?

Using a subjective scale ranging from 1 (low) to 10 (high) – how do you rate yourself on:

1. Connecting to people from other cultures

2. Performing in my intercultural work

3. Enjoying my intercultural interactions

Which of the three aspects do you want to improve right now?

My current priority: _____

Which of your IRC strengths could you use to improve the aspect of intercultural effectiveness you consider most important?

_____

_____

Which of your IRC pitfalls do you want to start addressing?

_____

_____

Using the suggestions for development: what specifically can you do to improve your approach in these areas?

_____

_____

5

Intercultural Competences Develop by Themselves: True or False?

Spending time abroad is important in order to develop intercultural competences – but it won't develop them all by itself. They're not like a suntan that happens just from being in the sun! To be effective and at ease in dealing with other cultures, we need to build on our abilities to listen, respond to signals, make and maintain networks and manage the newness of places and people strange to us. And the key to intercultural competence is our cross-cultural friendships.

There are many myths about working and living in other cultures – and our research has found some startling results, vindicating some ideas and absolutely disproving others.

Global organizations increasingly need internationally-oriented employees who are willing and able to work across cultures. In selecting applicants, organizations look for clues about mobility, favouring applicants who stayed abroad over those who stayed home. Applicants know that their experience abroad demonstrates their potential for performing in a global organization, and that it is best to present it as a positive experience, a unique opportunity for development.

When it comes to sending people abroad, the candidate's exposure to other cultures is decisive. Some people will adapt and return home having improved their CV. Others may fail to adapt when they get there. How do you explain who succeeds and who fails? This is difficult when it comes to expatriation, and so organizations may be tempted to rely on the 'sink or swim' concept: the idea that people who have a knack for the global challenge will survive, and those who lack it will fail. Either way, corporations assume that prior exposure to other cultures is an accurate measure of future success in working in different countries.[1]

There is little agreement about what it means to be interculturally effective.[2] In the absence of any effectiveness criteria firmly ingrained in selection and development processes, a myth has developed about cross-cultural exposure. This myth is that 'exposure equals competence'. According to this belief, people are interculturally competent because they have spent time abroad, or they develop whatever competences they need simply by starting to work with people from other cultures. The 'exposure equals competence' belief equates cross-cultural exposure with being interculturally competent, and it lures decision-makers into looking for evidence of cross-cultural experience rather than measuring and developing intercultural competences.

But the results of all our tests are unequivocal: people do not become interculturally competent simply by spending time abroad, or being exposed to cultural differences in other ways. What our tests reveal is something different: those who have built meaningful relationships with people from other cultures, either at work or in their private lives, have a head-start in intercultural competence development – regardless of whether they have lived abroad.

The 'Exposure Equals Competence' Myth

Many organizations invest in intercultural competence development. They offer pre-departure training to expatriates and international students; hire intercultural professionals for cross-border M&A integration programmes; invest in training in order for staff members to develop their cross-cultural communication and negotiation skills, their ability to work in multicultural teams and to lead a culturally diverse work force. But how great is this investment, and this commitment, really?

The size of investments in intercultural competence development has been studied best in the corporate expatriation market. At first sight, the numbers reported in these studies suggest large-scale investments. The authoritative *Global Relocation Trends: 2012 Survey Report*, published by Brookfield Global Relocation Services, finds that 83 per cent of companies with staff on foreign assignments offer pre-departure training.[3] This is an impressive percentage. However, Brookfield also reports that more than half of these companies make the availability of pre-departure training dependent on the perceived cultural novelty or cultural distance between the expatriate's home country and the country to which they are travelling.

The study also found an unexpected trend among European companies. The creation of a single internal market in the European Union (EU) in January 1993, which involves the free movement of goods, services, capital and people within EU countries, has apparently had an unexpected side-effect for expatriates: according to the Brookfield report, many European companies now consider inter-European assignments as *local* assignments, that is, as assignments that do not involve a change of country or culture. While it is true that EU citizens are free to take up work in any of the other member states, a political achievement as recent as the 20-year-old European internal market has scarcely levelled out cultural differences that have been in existence for hundreds of years.[4]

Finding and preparing staff for expatriate assignments is one of the toughest challenges for organizations operating globally. Typically, organizations do not have the luxury of selecting from several candidates those who are interculturally most competent, since finding even a single volunteer who can move, given his or her current career and family situation, already presents an obstacle.

Hilary Harris and Chris Brewster, specialists in international management, say that decision-makers may feel unable to determine from afar what exactly a foreign position should involve, in terms of the personal, professional and managerial qualifications of the person who will hold the job. This makes it hard for managers to calmly and rationally go about assessing someone for a posting abroad.

The difficulty of finding and selecting suitable candidates leads decision-makers to apply a selection process which Harris and Brewster aptly call the 'coffee-machine system'. In their 1999 study of multinational corporations, 'The Coffee-Machine System: How International Selection Really Works', the authors set out what they describe as the reality of international selection.[5] During a chat at the coffee machine, a line manager mentions how urgently they are looking for someone to fall in for the guy in India, and a colleague mentions that Simon from the fifth floor was on vacation in Goa with his wife a couple of years ago and apparently liked it. Simon is then approached for the posting in India, warms up to the idea and, from then on, all official screening processes are applied backwards to justify a decision that has already been taken. All that is left for the HR department to do is to assist with the paperwork. A holiday in Goa or a vague interest in the country under discussion is embraced as a reason to have a chat with Simon, and to then remove all obstacles that might cause Simon to change his mind.

Having found a candidate through sheer luck, how could one risk losing him or her through rational intercultural competence assessment? And with all the frantic preparation and paperwork required for ensuring a safe move for Simon and his family, what time and mental space are left for Simon and his partner to develop their intercultural competences?

We do not want to belittle in any way the enormous challenges faced by all parties involved at each step in expatriation. But there is a real risk of responding to such difficulties with a psychological reflex of *denying* that intercultural competences must be developed, and must be developed in time before any assignment starts.

While expatriation is probably the most challenging of all intercultural work endeavours for expatriates, their partners and families and their organization, it is not the only situation at work for which staff need to be interculturally competent. How many of the millions of people involved in cross-border work are prepared for the intercultural aspect of their job? Have you been trained in this?

The need for intercultural competence development for today's global professionals is widely underestimated. This conclusion is inevitable once we look at reports – other than those on expatriation – on how companies define what is required for the jobs they are offering. We will look at three representative sources of information on what the world of work requires of those who are in it.

The Occupational Information Network

One source is the Occupational Information Network, abbreviated as O*NET, developed by the US National Center for O*NET Development.[6] O*NET is a freely accessible online database developed for the US labour market, which describes jobs and their requirements in the US. If you wonder which job works best for you, you can find information on hundreds of career tracks, the skills and knowledge you need for them, what your tasks will look like and how much money you can make.

O*NET is based on a classification of 150 million jobs in the US labour market, categorized according to the US Standard Occupation Classification system into 1110 occupations. Of the 1110 occupations, 974 are specified more closely through over 275 standardized and occupation-specific information packages called 'descriptors', which detail the nature of the job, and what the job-holder needs to do the work. For example, if your daughter wants to become a water resource specialist, she will see on O*NET that her tasks may involve developing plans to protect watershed health or rehabilitate watersheds, that her tools will likely range from water samplers to software, that she should know her chemistry, physics and geography, and be skilled in complex problem-solving, critical thinking and systems evaluation.[7]

O*NET works with seven main categories of job descriptors, including abilities, interests, knowledge and skills. It lists 52 specific abilities (for instance, cognitive abilities like deductive reasoning), 30 interest areas (such as social and artistic interests), 33 knowledge areas (such as physics and geography) and 35 skills (for example, social and technical skills). The overall system is extremely clear and systematic, yet it does not present today's world of work as one to which intercultural competences hold the key. We did not find a single reference to something akin to intercultural competences amongst the 52 abilities or 35 skills. We did, however, find a reference in one of the 33 knowledge areas – as knowledge of sociology and anthropology, defined as 'knowledge of group behaviour and dynamics, societal trends and influences, human migrations, ethnicity, cultures and their history and origins'. For more than 300 of the 974 occupations described by O*NET – that is, more than a third of all occupations – the category is either not available or considered irrelevant. O*NET lists a top 30 of occupations for which knowledge of sociology and anthropology is important. These 30 occupations are practically all jobs in teaching and counselling, but not jobs typical of today's global workers, who need to be interculturally effective as engineers, in sales, production or accounting.[8] With 38 million immigrants living in the US, and more than 300,000 US firms engaged in international trade, this sparse attention to intercultural competences is a surprise.[9]

Quantifying Skill Needs in Europe

In Europe, the situation is very much the same. The European Centre for the Development of Vocational Training (CEDEFOP), in its 2013 report, *Quantifying Skill Needs in Europe: Occupational Skills Profiles: Methodology and Application*, does not list a single intercultural competence as relevant for a job, even though the report aims to cover the skill profiles of 240 million jobs in 29 European countries.[10]

The report does, however, mention a competence called 'general culture/ cultural awareness and expression' as one of eight key competences for lifelong learning. The competence is defined as 'appreciation of the importance of the creative expression of ideas, experiences and emotions in a range of media, including music, performing arts, literature, and the visual arts'.[11] That is, the meaning of 'culture' underlying this competence is 'culture as art' rather than 'culture as a way in which a group of people has been organizing its life'. The competence is not seen as an *intercultural competence*, meaning the ability to understand the perspective of people from a culture other than one's own, and to empathize, communicate and cooperate with them.

The CEDEFOP report does not mention a single intercultural competence on any of its 144 pages – even though, across Europe, Germany alone has more than 110,000 firms engaged in cross-border trade, the United Kingdom sends out 3 million expatriates, and more than half of Amsterdam's population is of non-Dutch origin.[12]

Developing Key Competences at School in Europe

Let us digest one more tell-tale European document, which alerts us to the competences that the next generation of global workers is expected to develop at school. The European Commission report, *Developing Key Competences at School in Europe: Challenges and Opportunities for Policy*, considers key competences to be 'essential skills and attitudes for young Europeans to succeed not only in today's economy and modern society but also in their personal lives'.[13] The earlier mentioned competence 'cultural awareness and expression' is listed here, too, as one of eight key competences, next to the ability 1) to communicate in one's mother tongue, 2) to speak foreign languages, 3) to be competent in mathematics, science and technology, 4) to be skilled in information technology, 5) to have social and civic competences, 6) to have a sense of initiative and entrepreneurship and 7) to have the capacity to learn how to learn. Again, no reference is made to an intercultural competence – but let us look at the fate of 'cultural awareness and expression', whose name at least reminds us of it. The report shows how often schools in various European countries taught the eight competences for lifelong learning. While six of the eight competences are reflected in the schools' curricula to a greater or lesser degree – among them the teaching of foreign languages – none of the schools seems to have given any attention to cultural awareness and expression. Throughout the entire report, the competence is mentioned no further.

Lopsided Attention: Languages versus Culture

All three of these documents explicitly point to the need for people to know and speak foreign languages. O*NET, for example, lists this as a separate category, and the schools investigated in the European report all teach foreign languages. But would it not be safe to assume – except perhaps for multilingual places like Switzerland, Belgium and the Faroe Islands – that whenever we use a foreign language, we are likely to be talking with someone from another culture? How much easier could our intercultural encounters be if we had already learned at school some strategies for connecting and communicating with people from other cultures, whose expectations, sensitivities and needs may differ from ours? Again and again, however, institutions keep investing in language skills only, instead of investing in both language and intercultural skills. A recent example of this lopsided attention is provided by Germany's MobiPro-EU programme, described in Box 5.1.

BOX 5.1 THE MOBIPRO-EU PROGRAMME: FIGHTING YOUTH UNEMPLOYMENT IN EUROPE[14]

In response to youth unemployment rates of over 50 per cent in several EU countries, the German Federal Ministry of Labour and Social Affairs invests about €140 million into MobiPro-EU, a programme which started in January 2013 and is scheduled to end in December 2016. MobiPro-EU covers language training and travel costs for people aged between 18 and 35 who want to move to Germany to start a professional education, or to work in organizations such as hospitals and nursing homes, where their skills are urgently needed. None of the €140 million is invested in intercultural training, which could support both the newcomers and their colleagues-to-be in understanding each other's needs, backgrounds, goals and intentions. What is the likely outcome of MobiPro-EU?

OECD migration expert, Thomas Liebig, told the weekly German newspaper, *Die ZEIT,* in 2013: 'Only about 40 per cent of the EU migrants who came to Germany in 2011 were still here at the end of 2012. Half of the Greek migrants changed their minds within a year, and of the Spanish migrants only a third stayed longer than 12 months.'[15]

The European Commission's Directorate-General for Translation 2009 report, *The Size of the Language Industry in the EU*, estimates that each year educational institutions and organizations in Europe spend €1.6 billion on the teaching of foreign languages.[16] If the same amount were invested in intercultural competence development, a whole lot could be done for getting Europeans who work across cultures ready for their intercultural challenge.

The myth that 'exposure equals competence' and that there is no need to invest in people's intercultural competences, is deeply ingrained in the logic of our educational and vocational training, selection and development systems. And it is time to debunk it.

'Exposure Equals Competence': The Evidence

Let us take a closer look at the 'exposure equals competence' belief. What would we predict if exposure indeed equalled competence? We will discuss four predictions derived from the 'exposure equals competence' belief, which we tested using the Intercultural Readiness Check (IRC) database:

1. **The generational prediction**: 'Today's generation of young people are more interculturally competent than older generations'.
2. **The regional diversity prediction**: 'Europeans are more interculturally competent than US Americans since Europe is culturally more diverse than the US'.
3. **The in-country diversity prediction**: 'People from culturally diverse countries are more interculturally competent than people from less culturally diverse countries'.
4. **The previous-experience-abroad prediction**: 'People who have lived abroad are interculturally competent'.

The Generational Prediction

If exposure equalled competence, younger people should be more interculturally competent than older people. Many people now in their late teens and early twenties have had considerable cross-cultural exposure through travel, the internet, social media and study-abroad programmes. It has become quite popular, for example, to take a gap year – a time-out between finishing school and starting to work or study. Many students use the gap year to spend time abroad, some of them with amazing results. We have recently heard of a Dutch student who went to Peru, where he realized that the beautifully coloured fabrics the Peruvians use for their clothing could also be used for making shoes. He now runs a company producing colourful sneakers that are hand-made in Cuczo, Peru, and sells them with great success through his website www.mipacha.com.[17]

Not all gap years lead to the creation of a business, but many of them are followed by a study-abroad period, financed, for example, through the EU's Erasmus programme, which celebrated its 25th anniversary in 2012. Each year, more than 230,000 students embrace the opportunity to study abroad in a European country through Erasmus. Before, during and after their time abroad, students can establish and maintain connections to like-minded people in other countries, all of which should give people of this generation a head-start in intercultural competences – if exposure equalled competence.[18]

With all these opportunities for cross-cultural exposure and connections, and all else being equal, younger members of the current workforce should have better IRC competence scores than older members of the workforce.

We tested this prediction using the data we have been collecting with the IRC since 2002. From 2002 to 2012, 27,290 respondents filled in the IRC to assess their intercultural competences. For three of the four IRC competences – Intercultural Sensitivity, Building Commitment and Managing Uncertainty – we could include the input from all of the respondents in the current analysis. The scale assessing the competence Intercultural Communication has been in place in its current form only since 2010; for this scale, we have data from 12,250 people.

Table 5.1 shows the IRC results for five different age groups. The overall effect of age is small; it is relevant only for three of the four competences – Intercultural Communication, Building Commitment and Managing Uncertainty.[19]

Table 5.1   IRC competence scores for five age groups

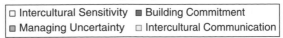

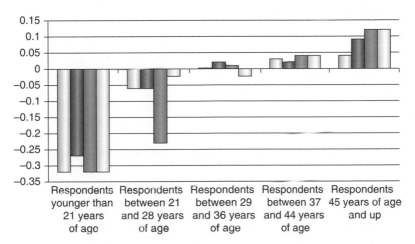

Table 5.1 shows the average scores on the four IRC competences for five different age groups. The youngest age group, aged under 21, has the lowest competence scores of all age groups on all four IRC competences. The oldest age group, people of 45 or older, scores highest on all competences.

Contrary to the generational prediction, the youngest age group, with people younger than 21, has the *lowest* scores on all four competences. The next group, aged between 21 and 28, has somewhat better results, but still scores lower than all of the following three age groups. Thus, the effect of age is the *opposite* of what the generational prediction would lead us to expect: what we find is that, contrary to prediction, younger members of the workforce have *lower* competence scores in important areas of intercultural competence than older members of the workforce. The generational prediction, according to which younger people, through enhanced exposure to other cultures, should be more interculturally competent than older people, is not supported by these findings.

But is it fair to compare younger respondents with older ones? After all, people who are in their thirties, forties and fifties have had more time to travel, live and work abroad than people in their teens and twenties. They simply have had more time for being exposed to other cultures, and this may be why members of these later age groups, in the end, are more interculturally competent than younger respondents.

To have a fairer and better test, we ran a second analysis, in which we excluded the later age groups. This second test allowed us to take large differences in age, with the accruing opportunities for spending time abroad, out of the equation.

The Generational Prediction (2): The Cohort Approach

To test the generational prediction in a better way, we compared different *cohorts* of respondents. That is, we compared the IRC results of people who were all at the same age when they filled in the IRC, but who filled it in at different points over the past years: in 2002/3, in 2007 and in 2012.

If people indeed become more interculturally competent through cross-cultural exposure that is made possible through travel, internet, study exchange programmes and social media, then people who were in their teens or twenties in 2012 should be more competent than people who were in their teens and twenties five and ten years earlier. Back then, people were less exposed to other cultures. The earliest cohort assessed their intercultural competences in 2002/3 – at a time when Facebook had not even been invented, and international travel was far less common.[20]

We looked at the three cohorts of people aged between 21 and 28 to find out whether those who were in their twenties in 2012 are more interculturally competent than those who were in their twenties in 2002/03 and 2007 – and so to get an idea of whether greater cross-cultural exposure has made people in the 2012 cohort interculturally more competent (see Table 5.2).

For the test of the prediction we had answers from 298 respondents of the 2002/03 cohort, 213 respondents of the 2007 cohort and 473

Table 5.2   IRC competence scores for three cohorts of 21- to 28-year-old respondents

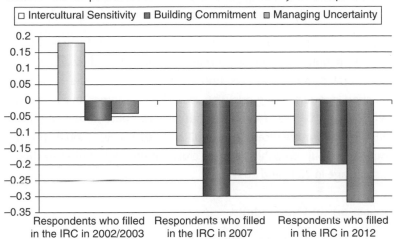

Table 5.2 shows the results on Intercultural Sensitivity, Building Commitment and Managing Uncertainty for three cohorts of respondents. All respondents were aged between 21 and 28 when they filled in the IRC, but took the IRC at different points in time: in 2002/03, 2007 and 2012. Higher scores indicate better developed IRC competences.

respondents of the 2012 cohort. Since the current scale assessing Intercultural Communication has been in place only since 2010, it is not included here.

Counter to what the generational prediction would lead us to expect, the 2002/03 cohort has the best results of all: people who were in their twenties in 2002/03 have *higher* IRC scores than those of the same age who assessed their competences five and ten years later. For Intercultural Sensitivity and Managing Uncertainty, the differences are significant: respondents from the 2002/03 cohort score better on Intercultural Sensitivity than people of both the 2007 and 2012 cohorts, and better on Managing Uncertainty than the 2012 cohort.[21]

These results fail to support the generational prediction. The 'exposure equals competence' belief would forecast that younger members of the workforce, who have had greater exposure to other cultures, should be more interculturally competent than older members of the workforce.

When we compare the intercultural competences of three different groups of people who were all in their twenties when they assessed their intercultural competences, we find no evidence that the generational prediction is correct. The group who took the IRC more than a decade ago, in 2002 and 2003 was more interculturally competent than the groups who filled it in more recently, in 2007 and 2012, even though this most competent group probably had less cross-culture exposure than those of the same age in 2007 and 2012.

Implications of Our Findings

The first prediction derived from the 'exposure equals competence' belief could not be supported. We found that older members of the workforce are more interculturally competent than younger members, and people who were in their twenties in 2002/3 were more interculturally competent than people who were in their twenties in 2007 and 2012.

This is an important finding, with implications for stakeholders engaged in enhancing their organization's intercultural effectiveness. We will zoom in on what our findings imply for educational institutions, governments and HR decision-makers in particular.

Implications for Educational Institutions

Our results indicate that international students may find a stay abroad considerably more challenging and taxing than is suggested by existing stereotypes of the flexible and adaptive young. We spend time abroad for many reasons, and some of these reasons may make the experience especially difficult. A gap year, or attending school while staying with a local family, may be less demanding than studying at a foreign institution to get a prestigious diploma, or having to work in a foreign country because of soaring unemployment at home. To be interculturally effective, students need to be interculturally competent so that they can connect to new people, perform to achieve their goals, adjust and enjoy the experience. This may be really hard when they are alone and far from home, and not as interculturally competent as it was imagined that they would be.

For institutions involved in internationalizing higher education, our results imply that they need to prepare students carefully before they go abroad, to consistently support students from abroad, and to ensure that local students are integrated in the learning process – local students' intercultural competences, after all, will probably not suffice to offer a consistent and warm welcome to their fellow-students from abroad.

Teachers and support staff we have spoken to often observe that foreign students keep to themselves, forming small groups whose members all come from the same country. They pass their time abroad safely ensconced in these groups as if living in a submarine diving bell. Local students, too, may stick to their own group, dependent as they are on their group's acceptance, and not feel comfortable enough to make friends with their foreign fellow students.

If students do not mix across cultural and linguistic boundaries, they miss out on an important chance of becoming more interculturally competent. Educational institutions need to facilitate interaction between students from different countries and groups – as difficult as this may be. Professional facilitation of intercultural interaction will enhance students' chances to connect to students from other cultures and learn how to work together. In addition, educational institutions should systematically assess their students' learning needs to better understand how they can support these students.

Implications for Policymakers in Government

For governments attracting students and workers from abroad, our findings suggest that investing only in language learning for those coming to their country may, in the end, be money unwisely spent. Double the budget and invest in intercultural competence development as well – for both the new arrivals and the receiving organizations. This will help expatriates from China, Spain, Greece and so on, to hit the ground running and connect to their new colleagues, perform in their jobs and enjoy their time abroad.

Implications for Policymakers in Human Resources

For HR professionals committed to building a pool of global professionals, the current results indicate that references to time spent abroad in an applicant's CV may not be sufficiently informative. If a global mindset and mobility are vital to the organization, decision-makers should carefully assess the most promising applicants on their intercultural competences through proven tools and methods – both applicants who have been abroad and applicants who have not yet been abroad.

The 'Regional Diversity Prediction': Europeans are Interculturally More Competent than US Americans

If it were true that mere exposure to other cultures equalled intercultural competence, we should expect that people who live in a culturally diverse region should be more interculturally competent than people who live in a less diverse region: by having cultural diversity at their fingertips, so to speak, people have ample opportunity for getting to know other cultures and people, which should support them in developing their intercultural competences. We call this the 'regional diversity prediction'.

According to this prediction, Europeans should be more interculturally competent than US Americans. Europe is culturally highly diverse. With just 10 million square kilometres (40 per cent of which is Russia), Europe is commonly assumed to be the world's second smallest continent, but in fact it is not even a continent but merely a peninsula of the Eurasian continent. Yet this peninsula is home to some 55 different countries (the count depending on a number of factors – for example, on where one draws the geographical line, whether one includes Turkey and Azerbaijan, or considers the Svalbard and Jan Mayen islands as states separate from Norway).[22]

The United States has a land mass almost as large as that of Europe – 9.1 million square kilometres, not counting Hawaii and Alaska. Along its 12,034 kilometres of land boundary, the United States has only two neighbours: Canada to the north and Mexico to the south.[23] Compare this to Germany, which lies smack in the middle of Europe. With 348,672 square kilometres of land, Germany is the seventh biggest country in Europe, but still just 'slightly smaller than Montana', as the *CIA World Factbook* reminds us. With its 3790 kilometres, Germany's land boundaries are about a third of the United States, and yet the country has nine neighbours, most speaking different languages: Austria, Belgium, the Czech Republic, Denmark, France, Luxembourg, the Netherlands, Poland and Switzerland.

Europe's cultural diversity can perhaps best be gauged by considering that about 20 of the 55 European countries cover less than 50,000 square kilometres.[24] Living in one of these countries – for example, the Netherlands (about as big as Ohio) – can give you the sense of being on a diving board: take a good jump and you are abroad – in England, Ireland, France, Belgium, Denmark, Luxembourg or Germany.

Cultural diversity could be said to be a hallmark of European identity. But does it make its people interculturally more competent than the people of the United States, as the 'exposure equals competence' belief would predict? To find out, we compared the IRC results of 2709 US Americans with those of 16,936 Europeans on Intercultural Sensitivity, Building Commitment and Managing Uncertainty. For the Intercultural Communication measure, for which we have fewer respondents, we compared the results of 1737 US Americans with those of 7215 European respondents (see Table 5.3).

Table 5.3 shows that US American and European respondents differ most in their Intercultural Sensitivity scores. This is also the only difference where nationality has any effect worth considering from a statistical point of view. While the effect we found is small,[25] its direction goes against the 'regional diversity prediction', according to which people from a region as culturally diverse as Europe should be more interculturally competent than people from a less culturally diverse region like the United States.

Table 5.3   IRC competence scores for US American and European respondents

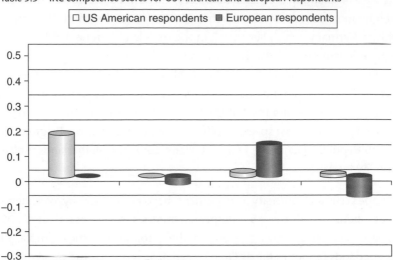

Table 5.3 compares the results on the four IRC competences for US American and European respondents, with higher scores representing better results on the competence in question.

Implications of Our Findings

Our analysis quite fails to support the commonly held belief that 'exposure equals competence'. People from culturally diverse regions are not interculturally more competent than people from culturally less diverse regions. We cannot rely on a region's cultural diversity as being sufficiently fertile ground on which intercultural competences will blossom. Instead, these competences must be honed and developed. At this stage, we can only speculate about why US American respondents score better on Intercultural Sensitivity than European respondents. As intercultural professionals, we are tempted to believe that the country's longer tradition of investments into intercultural training – which started with Edward T. Hall's work at the Foreign Service Institute in the early 1950s – is reflected in the results.[26]

One implication of our finding is that US Americans and Europeans may want to update the self-stereotypes of their intercultural savvy. In our work, we have come across US American participants who see themselves as less open and interested in other cultures than presumably more culturally sophisticated Europeans. European participants, on the other hand, may feel they have a head-start in the matter, that when it comes to dealing with different cultures, they are on their home turf. Our results show that neither of these self-stereotypes is justified. Intercultural professionals should support their clients in overcoming such unwarranted self-images so that these images don't get in their clients' way of developing their intercultural competences – wherever they may happen to start their individual journey.

Importantly, our findings do **not** imply that lack of cultural diversity is better for intercultural competence development. Such conclusions might be drawn by people who believe that diversity is so costly to a society that it should not be promoted. We firmly disagree with any line of argument in which supposedly valid calculations of diversity's costs to a society are used to argue in favour of cultural homogeneity in a society. Such a belief will not enable anyone to deal with today's realities or learn to constructively interact with members of different cultural groups, nor will it enable any society to deal with its diversity. What our findings do suggest is that effort and energy, time and money must be invested – by individuals and societies – for intercultural competences to be developed, at all levels and institutions in a society.

The 'In-Country Diversity Prediction'

So far, none of the predictions derived from the 'exposure equals competence' belief could be supported: neither the younger members of the workforce, with arguably more cross-cultural exposure, nor residents of culturally diverse regions like Europe, show any of the predicted elevations in their IRC scores. On the contrary: where we have found an effect worth mentioning from a statistical point of view, the effect was in favour of the opposite prediction. Older members of the workforce are more interculturally competent than younger members, earlier cohorts of people in their twenties were more interculturally competent than later cohorts, and US Americans are interculturally more sensitive than Europeans.

But perhaps regional cultural diversity, cornerstone of the last section, just does not translate into cross-cultural exposure? People may or may not decide to seek the cultural riches surrounding their country. Even though many European countries are small, this may not mean that their citizens constantly hop across borders to befriend their neighbours. In contrast, if their citizens do go abroad they often flock together on campsites and in tourist enclaves where local shops and restaurants cater to their every nation-specific need, and where they don't have to endure a single day without the comfort and food they are accustomed to. Regional diversity may be too crude a measure for testing whether exposure to other cultures builds the intercultural muscle.

Can we refine the regional prediction and zoom in on the cultural diversity *within* a country? That is, can we test whether citizens of culturally more diverse *countries* (rather than regions) have higher intercultural competence scores than citizens of culturally less diverse countries? Surely living in a culturally highly diverse country should allow its citizens to develop the intercultural mindset vital for today's world, because they can be in regular touch with fellow citizens from other cultural groups? This is the 'in-country diversity prediction' that follows from the 'exposure equals competence' belief: it posits that people from culturally diverse countries are more interculturally competent than people from culturally less diverse countries.

To test the 'in-country diversity prediction', we drew on three indicators of how culturally diverse a country is relative to other countries: the ethnic fractionalization index, the religious fractionalization index and the linguistic fractionalization index. The indices tell us how likely it is for people in a given country to meet a fellow-citizen who is of a different ethnicity or religion, or who speaks a different language (see Box 5.2 for an example of linguistic fractionalization in Belgium).[27]

BOX 5.2 LINGUISTIC FRACTIONALIZATION IN BELGIUM

Belgium, for example, has three official languages, French, Dutch and German, and so it is linguistically relatively fractionalized. While many Belgians are fluent in two or even all three languages, official occasions require paying due respect to each language group. One such occasion is a change in monarchy. On Sunday 21 July 2013, King Albert II of Belgium abdicated at the age of 79 after 20 years' reign, and his eldest son, 53-year-old Prince Philippe, was inaugurated as the new King of Belgium. The new king's address to the people was formulated in all three official languages, but the number of words per language differed, reflecting the number of citizens speaking the corresponding language. According to our word count of the text that was published on the website of *De Standaard*, one of the major Belgian daily newspapers, King Philippe's address contained 369 French words, 351 Dutch words and 38 German words – or, as we heard a speaker on the radio summarize it two days before the abdication, 'about 60 per cent of the address will be in Dutch, 40 per cent in French and then a bit of German'.[28] (Quote from memory.)

We tested the 'in-country diversity prediction' by correlating the average IRC scores of 23,705 respondents with the ranking of their country on the three fractionalization indices. Thirty-five countries for which we had sufficient data were listed in all three indices and so could be included in the analysis.

The combination of four competences and three indices yields 12 combinations we can test. If cultural diversity within a country indeed helps the country's citizens to build their intercultural competences through plenty of contact with their culturally different fellow-citizens, we would expect those 12 combinations to show a positive correlation – that is, a positive relationship between living in a highly diverse country and being interculturally competent.

This is not what we found. None of the 12 correlations reaches the threshold for being relevant. Nine of the 12 are far from reaching that threshold. Moreover, five of the nine correlations are *negative* correlations, and so indicate a negative relationship between living in a highly diverse country and being interculturally competent.

We also found such a negative relationship for the strongest of the 12 correlations, which is the correlation between Managing Uncertainty and ethnic fractionalization. This correlation does approach the minimum threshold for being relevant – but in the wrong direction, suggesting that people from countries with high cultural diversity find it *more* difficult to manage the uncertainty that comes with cross-cultural interactions than people from countries with less cultural diversity. This is in direct contrast to what the 'in-country diversity prediction' would lead us to expect.

Implications of Our Findings

We have seen that in-country diversity, captured through three different country indices – ethnic, religious and linguistic fractionalization – does not correspond to higher IRC competence scores. The findings are in line with our general argument that exposure alone does not make people interculturally competent, that something else needs to happen in addition to being near people from different cultural, ethnic, linguistic or religious groups. But to explain why in particular ethnic fractionalization correlates negatively with Managing Uncertainty, a closer look at the fractionalization indices themselves would be necessary – for example, whether these indices correlate with a country's socio-economic status, which in turn may influence people's ability to manage uncertainty. While such an analysis is beyond the scope of this chapter, how socio-economic factors may impact on people's ability to deal with cultural differences is an important question, and we hope that our analyses will encourage further research in this direction.

A Closer Look at 'Exposure Equals Competence'

None of the three predictions tested so far – the 'generational prediction', the 'regional diversity prediction' or the 'in-country diversity prediction' – has been supported by the data. This suggests that the assumption from which all three predictions have been derived is not correct – exposure just does not equal competence. Intercultural competences do not grow by themselves through cross-cultural exposure, but instead must be carefully honed and developed.

Why does exposure not equal competence? Intercultural competences probably do not develop in outer space: to become more interculturally competent, we need to interact with people from other cultures to some extent. Interaction involves exposure, so what's wrong with trusting exposure to do its job?

Exposure May Simply Mean Proximity Rather than Interaction

Exposure may simply mean *proximity* between people from different cultures, rather than actually engaging with culturally different others who live in the same country as ourselves, or across a border. Living in culturally-mixed Amsterdam does not necessarily mean we have to have contact with people from other groups. On the contrary: the better we know the city and how it functions, the more competently we can navigate around making contact – the area we choose to live in, the school we send the kids to, the streets we shop in, restaurants and cinemas we frequent may all be selected (consciously or unconsciously) so that we only need to deal with people like ourselves.

For people living abroad, exposure involves, of course, more than proximity; it involves regular face-to-face contact with people from the host country or other foreigners. International students, for example, will share the same classroom with students from the host country and with other international students; expatriates will have lots of interactions with both locals and other expatriates. This exposure has a great advantage over mere proximity, because exposure generally leads to liking. Many studies have demonstrated that when we see people (or things) for a second time, we are generally more positive about them than we were the first time (which is why so many advertisements on television are repeated).[29]

But liking is not the same as being interculturally competent. Many Germans like 'the Dutch', but despite liking their Dutch team, German managers may easily push all the wrong buttons with their Dutch co-workers the minute they instruct them in ways that are perfectly polite in a German business context (for example, 'Could you please finish that report by Monday?') but come across as too bossy in a Dutch context (in which something akin to 'This report . . . have you had a chance to look at it?' would be a strong enough signal). And how long will a manager continue to like their Dutch team if they meet continual resistance and ill-will without understanding where it comes from? While exposure leads to liking in principle, the general stress of expatriation, coupled with the interpersonal stress that builds up if we lack intercultural skills, can quickly do away with liking – on both sides.

There is an important benefit of exposure, a benefit which has been thoroughly investigated by researchers who wanted to understand how prejudice between two groups could be reduced. This research question, known as the 'contact hypothesis', was first proposed by psychologist Gordon Allport in his 1954 book, *The Nature of Prejudice*.[30] Psychologists Thomas F. Pettigrew and Linda R. Tropp, in their 2011 book *When Groups Meet*, unambiguously demonstrate, through a breathtaking meta-analysis involving data from more than 500 studies conducted since Allport's publication, that contact between groups reduces prejudice.[31]

While this is an important result, the evidence supporting the value of contact between groups does not support the 'exposure equals competence' myth.

First, many global professionals work with people from cultural groups towards which they did not acquire any particular prejudices through growing up in a country with its specific group conflicts and majority–minority issues.

Second, not being prejudiced is not the same as being interculturally competent. A global professional may have the most positive beliefs about Japan and the Japanese culture, but may still fail to effectively work with his Japanese co-workers because he lacks the necessary intercultural competences. We have worked with US American students in Paris, who were studying there for two summer months, and who had fought to persuade their worried parents to allow them to come to Paris at a time when relationships between the two countries were under strain during the Iraq crisis in 2004. But with all their love for the French culture, the students still had to pull together all their strength to sit still for two hours on wooden benches in rooms with no air conditioning, and to listen to their French professors, who saw their teaching style as part of the cultural experience the students had come to Paris for. They only had two months to develop a learning style that required them to be less actively involved and participative, but more patiently listening, digesting big chunks of information presented in a short time.

While contact reduces prejudice, wanting to make contact and failing to do so may actually throw our intercultural development into reverse. Psychologist Marian van Bakel, in her 2012 longitudinal study, *In Touch with the Dutch*, found that expatriates in the Netherlands who had no local contacts outside work became *less* open-minded over a period of nine months.[32] And there was nothing 'wrong' with these particular people that might have kept them from getting in touch with the Dutch. Contrary to popular stereotype, the Netherlands is a country in which it is fairly difficult for expatriates to make friends with locals.[33] While everyone speaks English, for instance, most people have a social schedule so busy that they cannot fit in meeting newcomers. A friend of ours, for example, once counted 24 family birthdays she had to attend each year, blocking almost half her annual weekends. (And she may very well need the remaining weekends for recovery.)

Proximity does not mean exposure or contact, and liking or absence of prejudice is not the same as being interculturally competent. So far, there is nothing to suggest that intercultural competences develop through mere exposure to other cultures.

The 'Previous-Experience-Abroad Prediction'

Marian van Bakel's finding that expatriates may become *less* open-minded as they spend more time in a country raises an important question: how do our intercultural competences develop as we spend more time abroad – do they always expand and grow, or could they possibly shrivel and shrink? This brings us to the fourth prediction that we derived from the 'exposure equals competence' belief, that is, the 'previous-experience-abroad prediction': the belief that people who have lived and worked abroad are interculturally competent.

If the 'exposure equals competence' assumption were correct, we would expect that once people have the opportunity to practise and polish their intercultural competences, these competences should develop in one direction only: upwards! Van Bakel's study, however, suggests that we may in fact become *less* interculturally competent through exposure to a foreign culture – perhaps because we cannot adjust to the culture, cannot find friends or have had bad experiences that keep troubling us because there is no one who could explain what happened, and what we could do differently in future.

Two studies suggest that the influence of experience abroad on people's intercultural competences, and on their effectiveness in cross-cultural work contexts, is negligible. Both studies are meta-analyses, meaning studies that pull together the results of numerous earlier studies, and so allow us to take a bird's-eye view, that precious angle from which we can picture the world without getting lost in detail and anecdotes. The two studies were published in 2005 by different teams of researchers.

'Input-Based and Time-Based Models of International Adjustment: Meta-Analytic Evidence and Theoretical Extensions' was published by organizational behaviour and HR management researchers Purnima Bhaskar-Shrinivas, David A. Harrison, Margaret A. Shaffer and Dora M. Luk. Their goal was to learn more about the factors that help expatriates adjust to a new country, and to find how being well adjusted would influence, for example, how expatriates perform in their jobs and how satisfied they are with their situation.[34] Bhaskar-Shrinivas and her colleagues combined the results of 66 earlier studies, which together involved data from 8474 expatriates.

What came out clearly was that relational skills, the clarity of the professional role and family adjustment make the difference: expatriates felt happier and more at ease the more socially skilled they were, the more clearly their role had been defined, and the better adjusted their partner and family felt in the new country and culture. We can confirm this from our own experience of coaching expatriates, many of them feeling guilty because their partner felt unhappy and not in the right place. And we have coached the non-working partners, who felt unhappy and lost because they had not defined their own egoistic goals for moving abroad. Not following our own goals, and only making partner and children happy, just does not work for very long.

Whether expatriates had lived abroad before did not play much of a role, Bhaskar-Shrinivas found: expatriates who had lived abroad before could only minimally benefit from this earlier experience as they adjusted to their current situation. The authors recommended that decision-makers should not use previous experience abroad as a criterion for selecting among expatriate candidates.

The second meta-analysis, 'Predicting Expatriate Job Performance for Selection Purposes: A Quantitative Review', was conducted by psychologists Stefan Mol, Marise Ph. Born, Madde E. Willemsen and Henk van der Molen. (We referred to their work in Chapter 3, when we discussed why intercultural sensitivity is so relevant for cross-cultural job performance.) Mol and his colleagues drew on the results of 30 studies which investigated, for a total of 4046 expatriates, the relationships between the expatriates' personality (for example, how conscientious and flexible they were) and how well they performed in their job.[35]

A range of factors predicted job performance, including someone's extroversion, emotional stability, flexibility and agreeableness, and intercultural skills like intercultural sensitivity, cultural flexibility and tolerance for ambiguity. Earlier experience abroad, however, did not predict job performance: expatriates who had lived abroad before did not perform any better on their current assignment than those expatriates who had never lived abroad before. Mol and his colleagues also recommended that one should not decide on one candidate over another depending on which of the two has already lived abroad.

Both meta-analyses suggest that the 'exposure equals competence' belief is incorrect. If you have never lived abroad before, but would like to do so soon, this is good news: apparently you haven't been missing much that would help you come to grips with the new situation or perform in the new job.

Or have you? Do people differ in what they make of their time abroad – do some of them benefit greatly while others return home less capable of succeeding a second time? The data available to these two teams of researchers did not reveal what people had learned and experienced during their earlier time abroad – participants of those earlier studies had merely been asked to indicate whether they had lived abroad before.

But there were clues suggesting the need to dig deeper and find out what actually happens to people when they live abroad. When taking a closer look at their data, Mol and his colleagues could see patterns suggesting hidden factors – such as the nature of the experience, contacts that were developed, events that happened. Take Jan, Financial Director of a Norwegian company, who went to Argentina on a two-year contract as Financial Director for the company's subsidiary. On arrival, he learned that his Argentine boss had already hired an Argentine Financial Director for exactly the same position. His boss and the Argentine colleagues considered the hiring of a Norwegian from headquarters as a clear sign of distrust; they felt deeply offended and disrespected. Jan's two years turned out to be extremely difficult.

While people are abroad, they experience positive and negative things; what they make of these experiences, and how they themselves can contribute to having more good than bad experiences, remains unclear if the only information is that they have been abroad. For some people, it's been a good time, for others it's been a bad time.

Across the whole group of expatriates, the positive and the negative effects may cancel each other out, so that when researchers only know *that* people have lived abroad, they cannot identify any benefits of that experience. The information 'has spent time abroad' functions as a cover term, hiding what factors truly play a role – factors that make expatriates more competent and effective, as well as factors that may make them less so.

Importantly, both studies suggest that exposure to other cultures alone is not a good enough criterion for expatriate selection – to say the very least, we need to know more about what attitudes and changes people may take away from having being abroad.

Insights from the IRC Database

So far, none of our analyses has supported the 'exposure equals competence' belief. Researchers who had other data at their disposal – such as Purnima Bhaskar-Shrinivas and Stefan Mol and their colleagues – likewise find no evidence that exposure, captured in terms of time spent abroad, plays a role: apparently, it neither helps people adjust nor perform better the next time around.

Do IRC competence scores show time spent abroad as having an effect – does it matter if we stay longer? If we know how intercultural competences develop as people spend more time abroad, we may better understand how and when they can benefit from earlier experiences, and how they might eventually use the experience to adjust and perform on a follow-up assignment. To find out about the effect of time abroad, we tested whether people have higher competence scores the longer they have stayed abroad.

But could we also analyse the IRC database in ways that help us to better understand what actually needs to happen while people live abroad? That is, can we unravel some of the factors that so far have been hiding behind the label 'has spent time abroad'?

To find out, we analysed the IRC database by combining three sources of information: IRC competence scores, how long people had already lived abroad and how many friends they had from other cultures.[36]

Why Did We Ask People about Their Friends from Other Cultures?

If we have lived abroad and made friends there, we have developed some very special relationships – relationships that are valuable and meaningful to us in different ways than relationships with colleagues, clients and acquaintances. When we develop friendships with foreign people they can help us understand their local cultural perspectives, feelings and sensitivities. For example, a German living in England had friends who just would not understand his jokes. But because they were friends, he could explain why the joke was funny; they had also agreed on warning signals indicating that a joke was coming.

Friendships survive tests even harsher than those involving humour: we can have an argument, a disagreement and even conflicts with friends, and learn from these because afterwards we're still friends and can talk about what happened. We can talk about events in great depth and with a great deal of trust; friends can give us a different perspective and feedback on our behaviour.

Perhaps we already picked up some ideas about how we should communicate differently – be more cautious, less direct or more confrontational than we would normally be in our native country or in our own work culture – but while we are still nowhere near perfection, friends can allow us to practise, and can give us valuable feedback without our risking the relationship because we just made a fool of ourselves.

With the IRC database we could test whether exposure to other cultures makes people more interculturally competent. By also probing for the effect of cross-cultural friendships, we could test which of the two is more important: spending time abroad or having friends from other cultures. And we could test whether the two interact with each other; that is, whether living abroad would affect people with few friends from other cultures differently than people with many friends from other cultures.

Cross-Cultural Friendship Beats Spending Time Abroad

What we found is that having friends from other cultures is vastly more important than spending time abroad. Cross-cultural friendship has a positive and substantial effect on all of the four intercultural competences assessed by the IRC: people with many friends from other cultures score significantly better on all IRC competences than people with few friends from other cultures. In contrast, having lived abroad has at most a very small effect or no effect at all on people's intercultural competences.

We found that when abroad, people with many friends from other cultures go through a different learning process than people with few friends from other cultures. While those with many friends from other cultures steadily develop or maintain their intercultural competence levels, those with few friends from other cultures lose what they have just learned when they spend more than a year abroad – their window of opportunity closes. Table 5.4 shows these results for the IRC competence Intercultural Sensitivity, and Table 5.5 shows these findings for the IRC competence Managing Uncertainty.

Table 5.4   Intercultural Sensitivity, friends from other cultures and time spent abroad

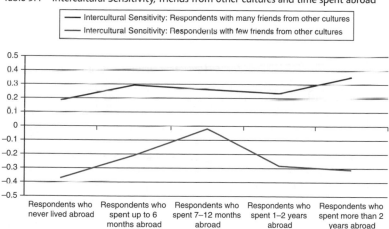

Table 5.4 shows the results on Intercultural Sensitivity and time spent abroad, for people with many versus few friends from other cultures, depending on how much time they spent abroad. Positive scores show that a group scores above average, negative scores show that it scores below average.

Research results from the IRC database demonstrate that people with many friends from other cultures are already interculturally very competent. Whatever living abroad can bring about in terms of intercultural development, they already tapped into that potential without leaving their home country. For three of the four IRC competences – Intercultural Sensitivity, Intercultural Communication and Managing Uncertainty – they need to spend more than two years abroad in order to measurably improve these competences any further. However, in the case of people who are rich in the competence Building Commitment, those with many friends from other cultures reap the benefit of living abroad within six months. This brings them to a level of competence that is not increased any further simply by staying abroad.

Table 5.5 shows the results on Managing Uncertainty and time spent abroad, for people with many versus few friends from other cultures, depending on how much time they spent abroad. Positive scores show that a group scores above average, negative scores show that it scores below average.

Table 5.5   Managing Uncertainty, friends from other cultures and time spent abroad

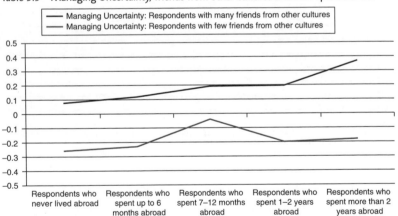

Implications of Our Findings

In using the IRC database for testing the effect of time spent abroad, the fourth prediction we derived from the 'exposure equals competence' belief, we found that cross-cultural friendships are vastly more important for intercultural competence development than spending time abroad. This finding has a number of important implications.

For individuals: if you are planning a career that involves expatriate assignments, you can prepare from home. Look around you: where in your professional and personal context can you meet people from other cultures? If you have organized your life in such a way that you move in circles of people who are similar to yourself, you will need to invest conscious effort into meeting others who are different from you. Look for networks with a culturally mixed member base. At home, you are a local – a member of that special species who can make a real difference to expatriates living in your country. Go and look for colleagues from other countries, and from other cultural groups within your country. Be the one who takes the first step.

If you are already living abroad, be realistic. If it is hard to make friends with local people, take extra effort to mix with foreigners from cultures other than your own. They, too, bring different perspectives and different experiences that can support you in developing your intercultural competences.

For organizations: create initiatives at work – both in the local headquarters and subsidiaries in other countries – for people from different cultures to meet, not just for work but also for non-work-related purposes. For work that needs to be done in groups, take extra care to create mixed groups – including both foreigners and people from different cultural groups living in the same country. Structure informal meetings to ensure that people mix. The 'similarity attracts' principle works like gravity: without effort or structure, we all tend to sit, stand and talk with people who are like us. Reward people who use their own initiative to spend time and effort to bring different people together.

Busting the 'Exposure Equals Competence' Assumption

Summing up, a thorough examination of what we call the 'exposure equals competence' belief proves that it is a flawed concept.

We tested four predictions derived from the 'exposure equals competence' belief: the generational prediction, the regional diversity prediction, the in-country diversity prediction and the previous-experience-abroad prediction. Our data on intercultural competence development, as well as data from other researchers, provide no evidence that the 'exposure equals competence' belief is justified:

1. Younger members of the workforce are not more interculturally competent than older members of the workforce, even though they can be argued to have substantial cross-cultural exposure. On the contrary: the youngest respondents in our database have the lowest scores of all age groups on the four IRC competences.

2. Europeans are not more interculturally competent than US Americans, even though they come from a region that is undeniably more culturally diverse than the US. On the contrary: the only effect we found that indicates any difference in intercultural competences between these two regions is in favour of US American respondents, who are interculturally somewhat more sensitive than European respondents.

3. People from culturally diverse countries are not more interculturally competent than people from culturally more homogeneous countries. Of the 12 correlations that we tested, approximately half showed that people from culturally more diverse countries tend to be less interculturally competent than those from more homogeneous countries. The strongest effect that we found likewise suggests that the opposite of what is predicted by the 'exposure equals competence' belief is correct: people from less diverse countries have higher scores on Managing Uncertainty than people from culturally more diverse countries.

4. Time spent in a foreign country does not have the effect one would expect if the 'exposure equals competence' belief were correct: across IRC competence scores, time spent abroad had a minimal effect on people's competence levels, and the effect of time abroad that we did find can be properly understood only if other, more potent factors are taken into account. In our analysis, this factor was the number of friends people have from other cultures: cross-cultural friendship is vastly more beneficial for developing one's intercultural competences than simply being exposed to other cultures.

Exercises

1) Find a pen-pal from another country; agree to write letters to each other every week for six weeks. In these letters, share your countries' local proverbs, swap recipes (and cook them and send each other photos and videos of you cooking the food and eating it with your friends or family). Tell each other the story of your first memory in school, and what happened when you lost your first teeth – did they have a tooth fairy put money under the pillow? Share information about your school clothes, your first dance. Tell each other jokes and explain what makes them funny. Share your taste in music with links to YouTube videos – and of yourself and your pen-pal singing or playing local music.

2) Sign up for some of the Skype conversation lessons given by native speakers. Talk in their language about things like what you both had for breakfast today, and what are the words in their language for odd things: galoshes, thingumajigs, whatshisname...

3) Somewhere in your town, hopefully, you will find an embassy or church or social group hosting 'Welcome to our country' meetings for lonely foreigners. Join up and talk to the people who come. Learn about their country. Invite them home for a meal. Bring them out to your favourite places for a walk. Make friends.

BOX 5.3 CASE STUDY: NO STRANGERS, ONLY FRIENDS

Pieter de Man – Regional General Manager Mid-Americas for Air France KLM

If there is an interculturally talented personality, it can often be seen in those who have spent their lives working from country to country around the world in multinationals. Some people have a talent for succeeding superbly in international commerce: driven, yet easy-going, happy with challenges, enjoying different customs and strange places. To people like this, no one is a stranger.

As Regional General Manager Air France KLM Mid-Americas, Pieter de Man is responsible for an area stretching from Guatemala all the way through Central America, Venezuela, Columbia, Ecuador and south through Peru. He is typical of the experienced and resourceful international executive.

Mr de Man has the perfect background for the job – he grew up travelling around the world, his father being Director of Public Works in Curacao, in the Caribbean, then with the World Bank in Washington, DC. Pieter had a mix of education: first 'a proper Dutch Christian school' in the Dutch Antilles, then US public schools and George Washington University.

'Not being walled into my own culture started with day one', he says. 'I've always been around all kinds of people; as a teenager, my friends were an international group, mainly Latin Americans. I grew up among that international community – World Bank, IMF, Inter-American Development Bank, all the embassies.'

He also learned business: as the family travelled back and forth between the US and the Netherlands, the teenager flipped burgers, ran his own swimming pool and worked as aide to a physiotherapist in a nursing home.

Then Pieter was drafted into the Dutch Army for national service. Here he got some of his best preparation for the international life: he was trained to be a counsellor, and learned to listen to adults talk about sometimes terrible problems, and then to try to help them.

He entered the army as a private and left as a commissioned officer, and went straight into his first job, with KLM. He has now worked with this company for 34 years. 'If you work for a company, you also have that company's culture,' he says. 'Air France KLM is a huge company culture: very, very proud, and loyal, and dedicated. Very much of a family feeling, an "us" feeling. You can be lost or demoralized, but it's the team that pulls you back up.'

This gave Mr de Man huge backing when he began his international career. After three years making his way through six departments in the Netherlands, he was posted to Qatar as District Manager, just before his 24th birthday, leaving behind his wife and six-week-old baby.

'I felt very lost, very strange, in a very different country with a very different culture. But that didn't last long.' His secretary was an Englishwoman married to an Egyptian, and she and her husband took the young executive under their wing and introduced him around – and helped him to get a visa for his wife to join him immediately.

'People were very kind and warm. At the beginning I had a little resistance – I wanted my world, my norms, my way. I was brought up that men don't kiss each other, don't hold hands for an hour and a half! But I learned, just did it, and learning new customs was pleasing, it was rewarding.'

One day the phone rang. It was a Qatari friend from the airport management. 'Are you home? I have a present for your children – go to the front door.' When Pieter opened the door, 'in a flash something passed by me – it was a baby goat. Such an honour, because in Bedouin tradition you count wealth in camels and goats.'

The family became friends with the KLM group, and then quickly with the expatriate circle, and outwards into the Qatari circle: the airport manager, immigration manager, customs.

The experience gave Mr de Man his basic template for learning new cultures, and when he moved next, to Bangkok in Thailand, he was able to find his way through this totally different culture. 'The secret was going with the flow a little bit, not trying to impose your own way and will and culture, but to listen and understand and respect and – when in Rome to act a little bit like the Romans. But a lot of it is about being yourself, being patient.

What's always helped me, too, is to at least learn a couple of sentences in the local languages – people like that.'

His next move was more difficult: back to the Netherlands. 'What a shock!' The family were now living in a suburb, and 'people weren't that open to having "foreigners" in the neighbourhood' – Pieter and his German wife always spoke English in the family, and must have seemed foreign to their new neighbours.

Next was five years in France. 'It took us a year before we acclimatized; we were living in a village. I'd travel in a typical week once or twice, leaving home at 5am or 6.30; home at 8pm. I'd travel to Marseilles, Nice, Toulouse, Bordeaux, Lyon, Alsace.'

They had kept the children in American schools all along, to have some continuity of language and education. So when their eldest was 14, the de Mans decided to move to Canada, and bought a house in Halifax, Nova Scotia. 'The idea was that I'd find the job of my dreams in Canada. I never found it – but I'm in my dream job in Air France KLM, and I stay with my family at least one week in six.'

After a ten-month stay in the Netherlands, Mr de Man moved on to South Africa – and its culture of 'lekker' (everything's 'lekker' in South Africa, meaning 'very nice'), and 'brai' (barbecues), and calling traffic lights 'robots'. He was Commercial Director for Africa, travelling through North, East and Central Africa – a whole continent of different cultures.

Then he moved to a new base in Nigeria. He was terrified at first – he went out and bought a cheap watch and a money clip for fear of robbers, but he was fantastically happy for his three-and-a-half years there. He was energized by challenges like sudden changes of airport landing charges, shortages of fuel despite ships standing offshore full of oil, and the horrifying lack of infrastructure.

'Once you have Africa in your blood you can't shake it,' he says. 'They are very warm and kind and open people.' After Nigeria, Mr de Man lived in Kenya as Regional General Manager Eastern Africa, covering a territory of thousands of kilometres, from Sudan, Djibouti and Ethiopia in the north down through

Uganda, Kenya, Rwanda and Burundi and Tanzania, and further south into Zambia and Malawi.

'It is a very diverse region, with Sudan, Djibouti and Ethiopia being very different to the rest of the countries. During my stay in Eastern Africa, KLM opened Khartoum, Addis Ababa, and Entebbe as new destinations. All very exciting. I had close contacts with the management of Kenya Airways, as Air France KLM is operating a joint venture to Europe with them. All in all, it was 12 super years in Africa.' Then he moved on again – to India, and now to Colombia.

Mr de Man has a firm idea of what makes someone culturally fluent, and what are the obstacles. 'A lot of people who are expatriates are so for a reason. People say "How can you live this life of uncertainty, confronted by different languages, cultures, dos and don'ts, insecurity?" What often stops people wanting to travel is that their spouse may have a good job, and if the spouse can't get a residence work permit in the new country, the family income isn't as great as you might have expected.'

It is not an easy life, he says. 'The French have a saying: "To part is like dying," and this is true. You're always leaving friends to go to a new place, and this always saddens you.'

But for those who love the expatriate life, a deep understanding compensates for the sorrow. 'People who work abroad need to understand what they're getting into. You don't do it for money, but for the people you meet, for the opportunity to be a world citizen.'

Key Points

- Spending time abroad does not turn you into an interculturally competent person without other factors
- Cross-cultural friendships are the key factor in enhancing cultural competence

- Choosing staff for relocation to other cultures must be done through stringent testing if it is to be a success
- The young are *not* more culturally competent than older workers
- People from culturally diverse countries are *not* more culturally competent than people from monolingual, monocultural countries
- Europeans are *not* more culturally competent than Americans.

6

Intercultural Competences for Culturally Diverse Teams

Cooperation can be hard both in the human and the animal world. A recent documentary on teamwork shows two chimpanzees who had to cooperate in order to get a banana.[1] They were in separate but neighbouring enclosures. Outside were two tables, each with a banana on it. The chimpanzees could pull the tables towards themselves if each pulled on a rope attached to one of the tables. Only if they both pulled their own rope at the same time would both tables move, and would each chimpanzee get hold of a banana. They could do that.

In the second round, only one table had a banana on it. To get it, the chimpanzees again had to pull their own rope, which they did, and the tables came within reach. One of the chimps was the lucky one – on his table lay the banana. He ate it. All of it. The other chimpanzee was beside himself, jumping up and down with fury. Chimpanzees can share and cooperate, but not when it comes to food.[2]

Witness to villainy, we felt sorry for the unlucky chimp, yet could not help laughing. But why laugh at such dire disappointment of a close relative? Because to us as human observers, it seemed so blatantly obvious what this unfair banana split meant – the end of teamwork. You win a banana, you lose an ally. Humans know that.

Teamwork – A Superb Human Capacity

The experiments shown in the documentary were conducted by psychologist Michael Tomasello and his team at the Max Planck Institute for Evolutionary Anthropology in Leipzig. The example of *human* teamwork shown in the documentary is mind-blowing – regatta sailing. Twelve people on deck; 12 different roles – each step, each grip and each word must be exact; each crew member must be able to fully trust the other 11 to be both willing and competent to do their job, and everybody must trust the group to function as a team. The wind, the direction of the waves, the movements of the other ships towards the finishing line – multiple factors to be calculated simultaneously to find the optimal route without bumping into other ships (where other people do similar calculations), and all factors to be translated into meticulously precise actions of 12 different people and personalities.

Harvesting the Benefits of Cultural Diversity

If human beings can achieve such extraordinary performance when working together as a team, why don't we do it all the time? And why, in particular, can we fail so dramatically when our team is culturally diverse?

This is one of the questions we will address in this chapter. The second question we will pursue is how teams can benefit from their differences, and how the Intercultural Readiness Check (IRC) can help them to do so. We shall consider this under four main topics:

1. What are the risks that culturally diverse teams face? We look at two studies showing the risks, and why teams cannot avoid these risks just by ignoring their cultural differences. If they ignore their differences, they will only be left with the costs and fail to seize the benefits of being different.
2. How can teams benefit from their cultural differences? Research on team diversity shows that teams can benefit from diversity only if they get a grip on their process: they need to manage the social and emotional dynamics in their team to avoid the risks of their differences,

and to expand their cognitive potential (perceiving, exploring and integrating different perspectives).

3. How can the individual capacities of team members help the team to get a grip on its process? We will look at studies showing how a team's belief in the value of its diversity positively influences the team process, helping teams not to fall apart into subgroups. We asked 4930 people who filled in the IRC to tell us about their diversity beliefs, and we found that the IRC competences predict how much value people see in diversity. Our respondents also told us whether they see subgroups in their teams. Our findings suggest that if *all* team members are interculturally competent, they can prevent their team from falling into subgroups. But there is only one IRC competence that helps a person to single-handedly reduce the risk of subgroups forming in his or her team. Building on these findings, we will show how the Intercultural Readiness Check helps to identify the learning and facilitation needs of culturally diverse teams.

4. With all this in mind, what can organizations, team leaders and team members do in order to get it right? We will summarize the key insights of this chapter by means of a seven-point action plan for culturally diverse teams.

Challenges for Culturally Diverse Teams

The world of work is becoming increasingly culturally diverse. Over the past three decades, the number of people who were employed by a transnational corporation has more than quadrupled. In 1982, transnational corporations had about 19.5 million people working for them; in 2008, they had 77 million employees. Within just a year, this number again increased by three million, with an estimated 80 million people employed by transnational corporations.[3] For many people today, working in a culturally diverse team is a daily reality.

Working in a culturally diverse team can be stimulating and exhilarating, and it can be really hard and exhausting. We want to perform, throw in all our energy and feel the rush of excitement of succeeding together. Then we notice the frowns on people's foreheads; they hesitate to applaud our brilliant ideas, ask us to repeat something simple or counter-argue in ways that have nothing to do with the point we made in the first place. They are lame in the heat of debate, or attack us for no good reason. They waste hours on small talk, or trample over all subtlety of human feeling. Cross-cultural teamwork is not for the faint-hearted.

BOX 6.1 WORKING IN CULTURALLY MIXED TEAMS

An example of the difficulty of working in multicultural teams comes from one of our clients, which has for several years organized programmes in which participants work together on a proposal for winning a major new customer – companies the size of Heineken or Microsoft.

For five days, participants work in culturally mixed teams. From collecting information about the target customer to presenting their proposal, participants have to take all hurdles towards developing a winning proposal during one intense week.

From the start, the teams struggle. It usually begins with language issues, which turn into communication and relationship issues, and eventually lead to frustration, conflict and loss of productivity.

A typical example would be one where the two native English speakers – John from England and Sue from Canada, for example – take the lead because speaking fast and fluently is not an issue for them. Feeling pressured for time, they hasten to tell the others what they think should happen. The Portuguese and the Spanish participants – let's call them Silvia and José – can follow what is said, but have no chance to intervene and bring in their own ideas. Hans, the Dutch guy, interrupts once in a while, but also fails to build up a longer argument and so eventually succumbs to asking critical questions.

José and Silvia need far more energy working in English than John and Sue because it is not their native language. Hans is doing OK because he is used to speaking English every day or because he doesn't mind improvizing. After a while, José and Silvia switch off; they stop paying attention, slouch a bit in their chairs and look elsewhere. John and Sue interpret these signals as lack of commitment, a failure to understand the urgency of the situation, and a failure to understand what they say. To make sure she's understood, Sue in mid-sentence starts telling José what he should do. That is, Sue has taken over assigning roles and responsibilities.

José, however, stopped listening 20 minutes ago. He doesn't have a clue what Sue is talking about and so just meekly says 'yes' as if by reflex.

José had a very different idea about how to start working together. He would have preferred taking more time to introduce each other, so as to find out about each other's background and experience, and how each could best contribute, given the nature of the assignment. He says 'yes' because the last thing he'd do is admit he doesn't know what John and Sue have been talking about; he would look stupid and unfit for the job. So José tries to figure out through the others what on earth he is supposed to do. This opens a separate channel of communication, and the team is starting to fall apart into separate groups, one group with the fast-talking and increasingly impatient native speakers, who have taken over the lead without any discussion about how the team should assign roles and responsibilities; and the other group of non-native speakers, who more or less succumb to doing what they are told to do. Hans may take sides, or may simply play along and do his job without really enjoying the teamwork or connecting to any of his teammates.

How much better this team might have worked together, and how much better the results for their project, if its members had worked on their cultural competences and were able to understand and communicate better.

Three Criteria of Team Performance

Teams need to perform by achieving measurable output in terms of the task they have been assigned – which might be maintaining operations, negotiating the best deal or developing new products and services, for example. The result of teamwork is often solely defined in terms of this measurable output: if a team has achieved its task-related goals, it is considered successful.

An example of this basic cooperation is a large Swedish food manufacturing company that brought together a group of Swedish content specialists and Indian IT specialists and web developers. The goal was to create an online learning platform for employees to continually update their knowledge of government regulations and industry standards. The bi-cultural team worked from two locations, Stockholm and Mumbai, and through some initial face-to-face meetings and intense phone and email contact, they did indeed deliver the platform in due time.

It is of course vital for teams to produce task-related output. But if organizations only use task-related output as a measure of team performance, they will overlook some real costs and potential assets of teamwork. To achieve any measurable output, team members first need to invest in their cooperation: they have to get to know each other and find out how each can contribute best, learn how to communicate effectively, coordinate their interaction and deal with potential conflicts. This is particularly hard work for members of culturally diverse teams.

If the team members are able to work together again in the future, all of these investments will pay off: the team will be much faster and more efficient in achieving output the next time around. Often, however, culturally diverse teams don't feel like working together again – but no one notices or asks why. These teams don't meet the second criterion of team performance, which is the team members' ability to work together again in the future.[4]

In the Swedish–Indian cooperation, the online learning platform was indeed built in time. After a great start, and real enthusiasm on both sides, the Indian team members started to feel that they did not really have a say in decisions, and could not convince the Swedish team members of their perspectives on visual layout, choice of colour and animations for the online platform. They were not employed by the company, and could easily get a new job on a different project with another company. So at some point, they simply gave up and played along, doing what the Swedish team members wanted. Perhaps it was because of the geographical distance to be covered, but the Swedish team members did not perceive their frustration, and failed to see that the Indians had given up on influencing decisions. They took the resulting harmony as a sign of their intercultural effectiveness, when in fact they had just missed a great opportunity to better understand how to cooperate with Indian IT colleagues on future projects. The organization lost the potential of having a team that works together seamlessly and efficiently, and can hit the ground running to deal with a follow-up assignment.

In the case of the Indian IT specialists, who were only hired on a project basis, the Swedish organization lost people who may have been very valuable in future company projects. If team members don't see their personal needs and ambitions satisfied through working with others, they may quit, or become de-motivated, losing the motivation to fully contribute at work. If this happens, their team has failed to meet the third criterion of team performance, which is the satisfaction of team members' individual needs and goals.[5]

In their 1998 landmark study, 'Demography and Diversity in Organizations: A Review of 40 Years of Research', Katherine Y. Williams and Charles A. O'Reilly show that diverse teams – where members differ in terms of culture or gender or in other ways – can indeed be effective in terms of *task-related* output, and may even outperform homogeneous teams.

Diverse teams, however, usually underperform in the other two areas of performance – in their ability to work together again, and in satisfying the personal needs of their members. Williams and O'Reilly reviewed 80 studies on team diversity and concluded that, overall, diverse teams have more turnover, more withdrawal and absenteeism; their members are more often excluded from communication networks outside the team, experience more stereotyping, are less satisfied and receive lower performance ratings than members of more homogeneous teams.[6]

While these results hold for teams where cultural or other differences play a role (gender or age, for example), a similar picture emerges if we only look at cultural differences in teams.

In their 2009 meta-analysis, 'Unraveling the Effects of Cultural Diversity in Teams: A Meta-Analysis of Research on Multicultural Work Groups', organizational behaviour and international management experts Günter K. Stahl, Martha L. Maznevski, Andreas Voigt and Karsten Jonsen identify recurring difficulties faced by culturally diverse teams. Members of culturally diverse teams feel less close and less attracted to one another than members of more homogeneous teams. Their morale is lower and they trust each other less than members of homogeneous teams do. Culturally diverse teams also experience more conflict than homogeneous teams, which makes them less effective, and they especially suffer from conflict when their job is complex and demanding.[7]

Considering the havoc that cultural differences can cause in a team, would it not logically be best to concentrate on what we all have in common instead of getting stuck on what makes us different? Teamwork, in the end, is about getting along with our fellow team members. We need to like and trust each other if we want to achieve our goals, and we need to avoid conflict, because conflict keeps us from achieving our goals.[8]

Ignoring our cultural differences, however, is not the way to go. As Christopher Wolsko and his team's study, 'Framing Interethnic Ideology: Effects of Multicultural and Color-Blind Perspectives on Judgments of Groups and Individuals', (discussed in Chapter 2) has shown, pretending there are no differences does not make us feel closer to one another, it doesn't help us be more accurate in perceiving where each of us is coming from, and it doesn't help us to acknowledge and appreciate that other people may have other goals and values.[9]

When it comes to teamwork, sweeping cultural differences under the carpet would have one particularly undesirable effect: teams would miss out on all the proven *benefits* of cultural differences that Stahl and his colleagues identified through their meta-analysis. Members of culturally mixed teams do feel less close and less attracted to one another – but they are also more satisfied with their cooperation if they succeed. And while they do experience more conflicts, culturally diverse teams also generate more creative ideas and develop more unexpected and innovative solutions than teams whose members all come from the same culture.[10]

Ignoring cultural differences does not make teams more creative or turn us into better team members – instead, we lose an opportunity for learning, connecting to others and generating more innovative ideas.

One of the studies demonstrating how culturally diverse teams lose their creative potential when they ignore their differences is described in Box 6.2.

BOX 6.2 CREATIVITY LOST

An example of creativity lost in culturally mixed teams comes from the research of psychologist Tina Girndt. In her doctoral thesis, 'Cultural Diversity and Work-Group Performance: Detecting the Rules', published in 2000, Girndt shows that when culturally diverse teams airbrush their differences instead of exploring them, they are no more creative than culturally more homogeneous teams.[11]

The teams participating in Girndt's experiments had to develop a challenging game that would appeal to young players regardless of where they came from. The games were evaluated both in terms of the originality of the ideas and their overall quality. There were 20 teams, most of them with four members and a few with three members. Ten teams had members from just one or two different cultures, and the other ten teams were made up of members who each came from a different culture. In the beginning, the culturally highly diverse teams did indeed suffer from their differences, in that they failed to kickstart into performance: they produced fewer ideas for the game than the culturally less diverse teams did. But surprisingly, the highly diverse teams quickly overcame their disadvantage – after a single hour of working together, they recovered from confusion and misunderstandings and continued to cooperate without further issues.

This is an extraordinary finding – but is it reason for optimism? According to Girndt, it is not. The mixed teams paid a price for their swift harmony, as the careful coding and analysis of their videotaped cooperation revealed. Again and again, the highly diverse teams had ignored verbal and nonverbal cues like repetitions and pauses, indicating misunderstandings. Importantly, the students misunderstood each other because they had different ideas about the game.

Since the students failed to detect these verbal and nonverbal cues, they brushed over their misunderstandings, and so failed to perceive, explore and integrate the different perspectives they initially had about the type of game they wanted to develop.

In the end, the culturally highly diverse teams had produced just as many creative ideas about game development as the less diverse teams had generated, but not more. The net result of cultural diversity for the teams in this study then was a cost: the loss of productivity in the beginning. They could not compensate for the cost by the benefit of being more creative – the teams had lost their potential for higher creativity that is so often celebrated as the hallmark of culturally diverse teams.

But how then, in the face of the undeniable difficulties that culturally diverse teams encounter, can we benefit from their potential? Insights come from research on diversity in teams – that is, diversity of any kind, cultural or otherwise.

How Teams Benefit from Their Cultural Differences

Research on team diversity has meticulously analysed what happens in diverse teams, and what these teams need in order to perform. Many of the findings resemble those on cultural differences in teams, but the level of detail reached in the broader field of team diversity functions like a magnifier for seeing what happens in culturally diverse teams.[12]

Any kinds of differences between people affect the team process in predictable ways, and by affecting the process, also affect team performance. Teams in which differences play a role can vastly outperform more homogeneous teams, but to do so, they must get a grip on their process: that is to say, diverse teams need to carefully manage the social and emotional dynamics affecting them so that their differences don't disrupt communication, increase conflicts and destroy cohesion. But diverse teams also need to pay extra attention to how they deal with information, and how they explore and integrate their different perspectives.

How do differences – cultural or otherwise – affect the team process? We'll first look at the nature of differences between people, and then at their effects on the team processes.

People: Which Differences Matter, When and Why?

Team members may differ in many ways from one another, and any one of their differences can influence their cooperation. Apart from nationality, differences in gender, ethnicity and age may affect them, just as differences in tenure and professional background may. Objective differences like gender can affect teams but so can subjective differences, that is, those that are perceived to be relevant, which are just imagined or highlighted on the spot. Humans are endlessly creative in imagining differences and similarities. Adults wearing braces on their teeth may find themselves in compassionate exchanges about material, colour and headaches with total strangers who likewise decided to get their teeth straightened. For a while, we drove a lovely chocolate-coloured Peugeot 404, a car with the squared charm of vehicles built in the sixties. On the highway, people driving Ford Mustangs, Corvettes or the occasional Oldsmobile Starfire would wave and smile at us, making us feel like members of a club we never knew existed.

While choice of car and dental measures can suffice to make us feel similar to some people and different from others, research on team diversity has mostly focused on studying the effects of visible (or surface) differences like gender, ethnicity and age, and those of hidden (or deep-level) differences like tenure and professional and educational background.[13]

At first sight, it is plausible to assume that team members benefit from diversity if they differ in terms of functional aspects like professional and educational background. This is the idea driving organizations to establish cross-functional teams, that is, teams in which specialists from different fields – for example, finance, marketing and production – join forces to ensure that they cover a multitude of perspectives when developing new products and services. But as organizational psychologists Daan van Knippenberg and Michaéla C. Schippers point out in their 2007 *Annual Review of Psychology* article, 'Work Group Diversity' (see note 12 above), functional differences can both help and hinder team process and performance, just as surface differences can help and hinder. According to research carried out by Hans van Dijk, Marloes L. van Engen and Daan van Knippenberg, what counts, apparently, is whether a given difference potentially matters for the team's performance.[14] A bodybuilder can contribute little to a cricket team, even though he differs from the cricket players in terms of functional aspects (muscle shape versus skill and coordination). But having people of different ethnic groups in the R&D team of a globally operating cosmetics company may be vital for developing a successful product range.

BOX 6.3 FOR WOMEN OF COLOUR[15]

Back in the sixties, established cosmetics companies were still entirely unaware of how badly their products fitted the needs of African American consumers, who had to devise complicated mixtures of products created for white skin to get the right foundation and make-up effects. But when Flori Roberts, a white US American journalist, overheard African American models exchanging tips on how to mix products, she realized she was on to something. Soon after, she started to work with dermatologists and beauticians on developing products for African American consumers, founded the company with her name and was the first white US American business person to serve customers who till then had been totally ignored and ill-understood by existing big companies in the cosmetics market.

The Social-Emotional Force: Processes in Teams (I)

The processes that matter in teamwork can be envisioned as two forces, impacting on each other.[16] There is the force of emotions and relationships between people: how we feel about ourselves and others; whether we feel safe or frustrated; whom we like or dislike, appreciate or ignore; whether we let disagreements turn into conflict, and how loyal, responsible and accountable we feel for the entire team. When it comes to this social-emotional force – the people-to-people link – diverse teams usually suffer. Like musicians from different disciplines playing together for the first time, diverse teams need to work particularly hard in order to coordinate their input and interaction.

Regardless of the nature of differences between people – surface or hidden, real or imagined – when it comes to this social-emotional force in the team process, two psychological principles need to be reckoned with.

First, we use real and imagined similarities and differences to distinguish ourselves from others, and to categorize ourselves and others as belonging to specific groups.[17] Left-handed people, for instance, can easily focus on how they differ from the majority, and partition the world into left-handed and right-handed people.

Second, regardless of which group we belong to, we usually like it better than others ('left-handed people use the right side of their brains, which makes us so creative!'). That is, we are usually biased in our perception of groups, seeing our own group, the in-group, in a more positive light than an out-group. When working together in a diverse team, we may, for example, more readily acknowledge and accept contributions from members of 'our' group than contributions from members of the 'other' group.[18]

When the two principles conspire – social categorization and in-group/out-group bias – teams fall apart into subgroups, and this subgroup formation is the real felon that's sneaked into the team.[19] For instance, we have heard of a female board member of a major Dutch IT company who came to meetings surprised to learn that her male colleagues had already decided on what had been discussed in the previous meeting. After a while she realized that after each official meeting, her male colleagues would wait for her to leave first and then go out to have a drink together. It was during the relaxed chats over a drink that decisions were taken. This team had failed to get a grip on the social-emotional aspects of its process and as a result, could not benefit from its potentially diverse perspectives.

A counter-example of a team that harvested the benefits of its diversity to achieve extraordinary results is given in Box 6.5.

In their 1998 *Academy of Management Review* article, 'Demographic Diversity and Faultlines', organizational behaviour experts Dora C. Lau and I. Keith Murnighan showed that the two principles kick in more quickly and strongly if differences between people conspire, creating a rift running through the team.[20] Imagine a team of three Romanian women in their thirties with a background in mathematics, and three Italian men in their fifties with a marketing background. Here, four ways of being different – gender, culture, age and educational background – conspire to create a very strong faultline with two homogeneous subgroups on either side. When this happens, all of the negative effects of team diversity – misunderstandings, 'us versus them' thinking, one-sided loyalties, lack of knowledge transfer – are likely to take effect, far outweighing whatever benefits diversity has to offer.

If differences conspire to create strong faultlines, all negative effects that a single difference can have on a team become amplified: we more quickly see each other as belonging to different groups, feel more one-sided attraction, are more biased in dealing with each other, feel less loyal to the whole team and have more conflicts. Faultlines in a diverse team intensify the negative effects of diversity, making it harder for the team to benefit from its diversity.

Cool Currents of Thinking: Processes in Teams (II)

Teams can benefit greatly from their (cultural) diversity: better decision-making, more creative ideas, more innovations. These benefits result from thinking, exploring perspectives and ideas, processing information and evaluating decisions from various angles – the people-to-task link. When diverse teams benefit from their differences, it happens here, where cognitive, informational aspects are involved: the cool currents of thinking.[21] Here, diversity brings two important benefits:

Diversity as a source of innovation and creativity. Team members differ in the relevant knowledge and perspectives they bring to the task. This by itself increases the chances that any *one* member will come up with the right solution, as in the example in Box 6.4. But as well as that, team members may build on each other's ideas and together as a team be more creative through exploring their different perspectives.

BOX 6.4 SHIFT IN PERSPECTIVE[22]

If you look around on your desk, chances are you will see an example of a product that resulted from diversity – Post-it notes! The story of how Post-its were invented is well known: Dr Spence Silver, a chemist at 3M, had invented weak adhesive glue – but for a long time, this seemed to be a 'solution looking for a problem'.

Silver originally thought of smearing the glue on vertical surfaces, allowing notes to be put there and removed again. It was years later that Art Fry, a new product development researcher at 3M, had the decisive idea. Fry sang in a church choir, and was constantly frustrated by the bookmarks falling out of his hymn books. With Silver's adhesive on them, these bookmarks would stick!

It was only because Fry's hobby required singing from hymn books which, unlike other books, stand upright when being used, that Post-its ended up handily on your desk. The story is an illustration of how, in a diverse team, in which members have learned to listen to their different perspectives, the chances that one team member will think of the solution are higher than in teams in which members are more alike.

Diversity as a constructive control mechanism. By evaluating a multitude of opinions and perspectives, teams can avoid premature consensus. A notorious danger of groups thinking aloud together is groupthink, which occurs when a group of people is too strongly motivated to keep harmony, too afraid to deviate, too anxious to avoid even constructive disagreement. The group then takes decisions that turn out badly and can be seen to be wrong once group pressure has ebbed away. Political decisions, like the US invasion of the Bay of Pigs in Cuba and the Allies' failure to foresee the attack on Pearl Harbor in World War II, and also corporate disasters like the collapse of Swissair, have been analysed as a result of groupthink.[23]

Avoiding premature consensus is thus extremely valuable to any team and organization. Groupthink is reduced in diverse teams, because when different perspectives clash, team members need to dig deeper to understand their divergent positions and deal with them. Through exploring diverse perspectives and arguments, weighing pros and cons, team members use the greater information available to them, and process it better. They take decisions that are more elaborated, grounded and thought through.

Ultimately, if diverse teams get their information processes right, team members can also stop and evaluate how they are working together, what they are supposed to achieve and how they should do it: should they aim for something else, and could all this be done differently and better?

To realize their potential, diverse teams need to get a grip on both processes: they need to carefully attend to their social-emotional processes, and simultaneously expand their ability to process information. It is how these two processes impact on each other over time, within the context of the team's task and the surrounding organization, that in the end determines whether diversity helps more than it hinders.[24]

Figure 6.1 shows a diagram of the two processes, and some key factors affecting teams.

The people working together are not the victims of their differences, or their task, or their organizational context. They can contribute vitally to making the cool current of thinking have the upper hand in their interaction. In the next section, we will discuss how the IRC competences can help predict a team's chance to get a grip on their process and benefit from their diversity (see Box 6.5 for an example of a team that achieved extraordinary results by harvesting the benefits of its diversity).

BOX 6.5 SABERMETRICS

Sabermetrics revolutionized baseball. Sabermetrics is the specialized analysis of baseball through objective evidence of what makes a winning team. Based on the acronym SABR, short for Society for American Baseball Research, Sabermetrics uses past and current contributions of players and teams to reliably predict their future contributions to winning the game.

In his 2003 book *Moneyball: The Art of Winning an Unfair Game*, journalist Michael Lewis tells the story of Billy Beane, General Manager of Oakland Athletics, who strategically uses Sabermetrics to buy affordable players and get the club back on the winning track.[25] Unconvinced of conventional methods of scouting talent, Beane followed his boss' suggestion and tried Sabermetrics. But the new approach only took off for Oakland Athletics when in 1999, Beane engaged Paul DePodesta, a cum laude graduate of Harvard with a degree in economics. DePodesta could have become rich on Wall Street but became fascinated by baseball because of its irrational assumptions and analyses, and the opportunities this offered. According to DePodesta, decision-makers in baseball over-relied, for example, on what they had seen with their own eyes; they overemphasized a player's most recent performance, and focused on player strengths and tactics without checking whether these actually predict future success. To DePodesta, baseball was a prime example of flawed human information processing. And to DePodesta, irrationality meant opportunity.[26]

DePodesta used new tools from the finance market to improve Sabermetrics, analysing minuscule aspects of players' performance and calculating their effects on a team's chance to win. These statistics painted a very different picture of what to look for in a player than what traditional baseball scouts had searched for.

No one wanted to listen to DePodesta except Billy Beane. And no one wanted to listen to Billy Beane either – that is, at first. But today, teams as big as the New York Mets and the Boston Red Sox have adopted Sabermetrics, with full-time analysts on their payroll.

Michael Lewis's book portrays Billy Beane as an intense and emotional man whose bursts of anger were feared and respected. He describes how, when Beane realized that scout Grady Fuson, despite all rational arguments and clear instructions to select college players only, had hired high school pitcher Jeremy Bonderman, Beane got up from his chair, and in a single fluid motion banged it so hard against the wall behind him that it broke into pieces, smashing the wall.[27] Yet, in his determination of winning without budget for top players, Billy Beane was and is cool-headed, and solely focused on what truly predicts victory in baseball. Conflict with coaches and scouts adhering to their old ways did not keep Beane from pushing Sabermetrics.

Beane and the economist DePodesta exemplify how a team can benefit from a new and different perspective – by concentrating on the task and not allowing conflict, emotions or relationships to get in its way.

By adopting Sabermetrics and bringing it closer to perfection, Oakland Athletics benefited from diversity and outperformed other teams, because it got a grip on its processes. With about $41 million in salary in 2002, Oakland Athletics safely competed with far richer teams such as the New York Yankees, with over $125 million in payroll during that season. That same year, Oakland Athletics smashed American League baseball's record of more than 100 years by winning 20 games in a row. In 2006, the team beat the dreaded Minnesota Twins in the American League Division Series. By now, Beane's commitment to Sabermetrics has paved the way for other low budget teams to reach the World Series.[28]

After the 2002 season, Beane received an offer from the Boston Red Sox of $12.5 million annual salary, the highest offer in baseball history till that date. He declined because he preferred to stay with his team.

Diversity Beliefs

Much of the more recent research on team diversity has focused on what people think about the diversity in their team. Do they like it, do they see value in it? Rather than looking from the outside, testing various factors of differences on team process and performance, many researchers in the field now want to understand how people's beliefs about their team's diversity influence process and performance. Often these beliefs are simply called 'diversity beliefs', which is the name we will also use.

Diversity beliefs are beliefs about the value of diversity for the team. Teams whose members are convinced that their differences will help them perform, will in fact get a grip on their processes and will indeed perform.

Where Do Positive Diversity Beliefs Come From?

What enables people to see the value of diversity for their team? One enabler is for team members to clearly see *how* their differences will help them perform. For example, in an experiment conducted by Daan van Knippenberg, S. Alexander Haslam and Michael J. Platow, published as part of their 2007 article, 'Unity through Diversity: Value-in-Diversity Beliefs, Work Group Diversity, and Group Identification', students were told that their team members differed in thinking styles. Half the students were told to generate as many *unique* ideas for solving a problem as possible, and that their different thinking styles would help them to do this. The other students were told that only their *shared* ideas would count for performance, that is, ideas that had been suggested by at least three of the four group members. No further information about the thinking styles was provided.

THE ORGANIZATIONAL CONTEXT

Organizational climate = Diversity as learning and integration? How diverse is the organization outside the team?

THE TASK CONTEXT

Do differences matter for performance? Cooperative interdependence? Degree of team autonomy? Degree of pressure?

The people about to work together and the diversity they bring to the team: Do differences conspire to create faultlines?	**THE TEAM PROCESS** Communication, conflict, cohesion	Team performance: Measurable output, ability to work together again, satisfaction of personal needs

People-to-task: Cool currents of thinking
Processing information and taking decisions

Diversity of resources and perspectives (information, knowledge, contacts outside, understanding customer needs)	Diversity as a positive control mechanism (pros and cons, better decisions)	Team reflexivity: Is this the best way to do this?	Team learning

Team identity: Feeling One

People-to-people: Social and emotional forces
Establishing and maintaining relationships among team members

Categorizing members into groups	Faultlines become activated	In-group/Out-group bias kicks in: *Us* is good, likeable and competent. *Them* is not	Conflicts between subgroups	Coalition formation

Individual attitudes and competences people bring to the team: Diversity beliefs, leadership style, intercultural competences

Time spent working together: Effects of diversity can change over time

FIG 6.1 People, process, performance – Key elements affecting diverse teams

The result: students who had to generate unique ideas, and were made to believe that their diversity would help them do so, were more positive about their group's diversity than the other students, and also identified more strongly with their team.[29] Experiments like these show that people can learn to value their team's diversity if they clearly see how it contributes to their team's performance.

But people may see value in diversity for many other reasons, for example, because they have already experienced success in a highly diverse team. People may see value in diversity because of their general attitudes and competences, for example, because they are particularly open-minded. Or they may believe in diversity because they are part of it. A second-generation Algerian immigrant in a traditional French corporation, or a woman in a male-dominated chemical company, bring diversity wherever they go, and easily see the value they bring. And people may value diversity because it is part of their professional identity – as is the case with intercultural professionals, whose very notion of being professional is inextricably linked to their belief in diversity.

What Makes Diversity Beliefs So Critical for Team Process and Performance?

Research on team diversity has shown that positive diversity beliefs have numerous positive consequences, helping people to get a grip on their team's processes. As psychologist Sebastian Stegmann wrote succinctly in his 2011 doctoral thesis, 'Engaging with Diversity of Social Units', diversity beliefs are both asset and buffer.[30] His meta-analysis of 50 studies on diversity beliefs in teams shows that positive diversity beliefs are an asset for teams because they help the team to process information (the cool currents of thinking become more powerful). Simultaneously, positive diversity beliefs work like a buffer, protecting teams from the detrimental effects of their differences: teams believing in the value of their diversity constructively manage their social-emotional processes, that is, they communicate better, have fewer conflicts and are less likely to fall into subgroups.

Box 6.6 gives some concrete examples of how diversity beliefs have been found to be both asset and buffer.

BOX 6.6 ASSET AND BUFFER: HOW DIVERSITY
BELIEFS SUPPORT TEAM PROCESS AND
PERFORMANCE

In his 2005 article, 'Having An Open Mind: The Impact of Openness to Experience on Interracial Attitudes and Impression Formation', organizational behaviour specialist, Francis J. Flynn shows that people who are open to diversity and new experiences formed more favourable impressions, and were less inclined to form negative stereotypes of other ethnic groups than people who were less open to diversity and new experiences.[31]

Psychologists Astrid Homan, Daan van Knippenberg, Gerben van Kleef and Carsten de Dreu, in their 2007 study, 'Bridging Faultlines by Valuing Diversity: Diversity Beliefs, Information Elaboration, and Performance in Diverse Work Groups', showed that team members who believe in the value of their diversity are better at exploring and analysing critical information than team members who do not see that value.[32]

As psychologists Karen van Oudenhoven-van der Zee, Paul Paulus, Menno Vos and Niveditha Parthasarathy demonstrated in their 2009 publication, 'The Impact of Group Composition and Attitudes Towards Diversity on Anticipated Outcomes of Diversity in Groups', if people see value in diversity, they expect more positive outcomes of diverse workgroups than people who do not see this value.[33]

Psychologists Van Knippenberg, Haslam and Platow, in their 2007 study, *Unity through Diversity*, show that positive diversity beliefs help team members to identify with their team as a whole, and so function like a buffer in helping the team stick together instead of falling into subgroups.[34]

One of the most intriguing examples of just how diversity beliefs help diverse teams to succeed comes from work by psychologists Astrid Homan, Lindred L. Greer, Karen A. Jehn and Lukas Koning. In their 2010 publication, 'Believing Shapes Seeing: The Impact of Diversity Beliefs on the Construal of Group Composition', they demonstrated that teams are immune to the risk of falling apart into subgroups even when faced with clear and present faultline danger – if they see value in their differences.[35]

In one of the studies demonstrating this effect (no subgroup perception despite objective faultline risk), Homan and her colleagues investigated 39 teams from a large Dutch financial organization. They classified the teams in terms of the objective differences in gender, ethnicity, tenure and educational background, and in terms of how much these differences conspired to create faultlines, which, as we have seen, increases the risk that differences lead to subgroups. All teams were also assessed in terms of how much they valued their diversity.

The key finding came from those teams with an objective risk of subgroup formation, where the four ways of being different conspired. (Imagine a team with two Dutch male economists who have been with the bank for 15 years, and two female insurance specialists from the UK who just recently joined.)

If the members of the high-risk teams valued their diversity, they reported that they did not see subgroups in their teams. In contrast, members of high risk teams who did *not* value their diversity clearly saw how their team had split into subgroups.

This is an amazing finding: the teams valuing their differences had turned a risky reality around, creating a better team reality. They did not focus on their group differences but on their individual differences, and they valued these. But in teams whose members did not value their diversity, the objective risk had crystallized into a negative team reality – these teams had fallen apart into subgroups, exactly as faultline theory predicts.

Diversity Beliefs and the Competences of the Intercultural Readiness Check

Given the pivotal role of positive diversity beliefs, we were keen to learn more about them. Would they be related to the intercultural competences assessed by the Intercultural Readiness Check? That is, would people who score high on the IRC competences also see value in diversity? This seems a plausible assumption to make, but it has to be tested nonetheless. If IRC competence scores help to predict people's diversity beliefs, then we could work with the Intercultural Readiness Check to identify for an existing team how much learning and support its members would need in order to get a grip on their team's processes.

We contacted Professor Astrid Homan and Professor Karen Jehn and asked them whether they would allow us to use two important measurement scales in our research: one scale, provided by Professor Homan, consists of four items assessing diversity beliefs, for example, 'diversity is an asset for teams'. The second scale, provided by Professor Jehn, consists of four items assessing 'subgroup perception', that is, how strongly people perceive subgroups in their teams, for example, 'the team I work in divides into subsets of people when working together'.[36] We are grateful to Professor Homan and Professor Jehn for their generosity in sharing their measurement scales with us.

In April 2011, we inserted the two short scales into the IRC online assessment process. Whenever people chose the English version of the Intercultural Readiness Check, they were invited to answer the two short scales as well. To avoid confusion, we clearly informed them that their answers to the two scales would not influence their results on the IRC.

By December 2012, 4930 people had filled in both the IRC and the diversity beliefs and subgroup perception scales, and had also provided information about their biographical background. About two-thirds of these respondents were men and one-third women. Respondents who had chosen English for filling in the questionnaire came from all over the English-speaking world, from New Zealand to Ireland, and from the US and Canada to the UK. Other nationalities were also included, with respondents coming from Italy and India, Poland and Pakistan, Sweden and Singapore, Turkey and Taiwan. Respondents differed in age, the time they had spent abroad and the time they had spent in their current function, and they differed in how many people reported to them.

Do Management Level and Time Abroad Affect Diversity Beliefs?

For two particular features of people's background – the time they had spent abroad and their management status – we tested whether these would predict people's diversity beliefs. We did not find any such correlation. That is, neither the amount of time people have spent abroad nor their level of managerial responsibility can predict how strongly they believe in the value of diversity for their teams. People who have been abroad for more than two years are just as likely to see value in diversity, or not to see that value, as are people who have never been abroad. Top managers with more than 50 people reporting to them are just as likely to see or to doubt the value of diversity for their teams as are people who are managing nobody but themselves. For organizations, these findings imply that they cannot just assume that senior managers with long-term experience abroad will be sufficiently convinced of the value that diversity can bring to their culturally diverse team.

Do Diversity Beliefs Differ Depending on People's Intercultural Competences?

While the two factors of 'time spent abroad' and 'management level' do not detect differences in diversity beliefs among this highly varied group of 4930 respondents, the IRC scores of respondents did detect such differences in certain people. We found clear and systematic relationships between people's IRC competence scores and their beliefs about diversity: the higher their IRC competence scores, the more they believe in the value of diversity for their teams.[37] The relationship was particularly strong for those with high competence in Building Commitment and Managing Uncertainty. Thus, while a high score on any IRC competence indicates positive diversity beliefs, people who are skilled in Building Commitment and Managing Uncertainty are particularly convinced that diversity adds value to their teams.

Our findings imply that organizations cannot just expect senior managers with long-term experience abroad to see value in their teams' diversity. Organizations, can, however, use the IRC for both team leaders and team members to assess how likely it is that the team will get a grip on its processes, and be able to perform.

A team leader scoring high on any of the four IRC competences, but especially on Building Commitment and Managing Uncertainty, will be very likely to see the value of diversity for his or her team from the outset. A team leader scoring low, in contrast, needs to first sort out and convince him or herself of the value that diversity can bring to performance. Only if the team leader is absolutely clear about why the team's diversity is essential for performance, should he or she start managing a (culturally) diverse team.

If all or most team members score high on the IRC, they are also likely to get a grip on their process and perform well. Recall the study that Astrid Homan and her colleagues conducted to test the effects of diversity beliefs on subgroup perception in 39 teams of a major Dutch banking institution. The study showed that when all team members believe in diversity, their teams are inoculated against the detrimental effects that differences can have for a team. In particular, the teams believing in the value of their differences were immune to the force through which differences lead to subgroups forming, with the destructive effect that subgroups can have on cooperation.

Our findings suggest that if all team members score high on the Intercultural Readiness Check, they will be inoculated against the force of subgroup formation. Their intercultural competences will work as a buffer against the detrimental effects of diversity on their team process; that is, an interculturally competent team is likely to communicate effectively, avoid conflicts and feel like one team. Team members' intercultural competences will help them to turn their differences into an asset, so that they will explore their different perspectives, refrain from premature consensus, be more creative and take better decisions. Highly developed intercultural competences in a team do not by themselves make the team more creative, but they enable team members to use the creativity they bring to the team, rather than getting lost in conflict and confusion.

Can a single interculturally competent person help a diverse team get a grip on its processes? In the study conducted by Homan and her colleagues, the whole team saw value in their diversity and so could benefit from it. Together they had created the right team reality. The study was not designed to test the impact that a single team member with strong positive diversity beliefs could have on a team.

There is, however, research on the positive impact that a single team member can have on a team, when they are the team leader. Astrid Homan and Lindred Green show, in their 2013 study, 'Considering Diversity: The Positive Effects of Considerate Leadership in Diverse Teams', that a considerate leader helps a diverse team to focus on individual differences and to function well.[38] The special impact of the team leader has also been demonstrated by Lynda Gratton, Andreas Voigt and Tamara J. Erickson, in their 2007 study, 'Bridging Faultlines in Diverse Teams'.[39] In 55 teams from 15 European and American companies, the authors analysed how two different leadership styles – a task-orientated style and a relationship-orientated style – affected the formation of subgroups. Neither leadership style in isolation could prevent subgroups from developing. Instead, only a combination of the two styles made a difference: those leaders who had started the team process with a task-orientated style to establish clear and shared procedures, and who then switched to a relationship-orientated style, getting to know team members better, had the best results of all. Their teams suffered the least from subgroups.

The effective leaders in the two studies probably all recognized the value of their team's diversity. But their diversity beliefs were only part of the approach they chose to use in leading their teams. It is still unclear then whether a single person can get a team on the right track purely because he or she believes in diversity or is interculturally highly competent.

IRC Competence Scores, Diversity Beliefs and Subgroup Perception

To find out about the possibility that a single team member's diversity beliefs and/or intercultural competences could steer the team in the right direction, we tested two correlations:

- the correlation between diversity beliefs and subgroup perception, and
- the correlation between IRC intercultural competences and subgroup perception.

If positive diversity beliefs of a single person would be enough to get an entire team on track, then a person with such beliefs would usually work in a team where subgroups had no chance to form and fester. This person's belief in diversity would be sufficient to keep a team from falling apart.

If a single person could have this effect, we would find a substantial correlation between people's belief in diversity and their perception of subgroups in their teams. Strong believers would overall report seeing no such subgroups – because they themselves had single-handedly kept those subgroups from developing. The doubtful respondents would more often report such subgroups, because they did not have the conviction that would have kept subgroups from taking shape. Similarly people with high cultural competence scores on the IRC would overall report seeing no subgroups in their teams since they themselves were interculturally competent enough to avoid allowing such cliques to form.

Would we then find a correlation between diversity beliefs, IRC competences and subgroup perception? We did, and the pattern is very interesting. Only one of the five potential subgroup preventers – positive diversity beliefs plus the four IRC competences – correlates with subgroup perception.

Positive diversity beliefs do not correlate with subgroup perception. And neither do Intercultural Sensitivity, Intercultural Communication and Building Commitment. That is, a single team member seeing value in diversity and scoring high on these three IRC competences all alone is unlikely to help prevent subgroups from forming.

If a single person with positive diversity beliefs and high scores on the three competences could prevent such subgroups forming in a team, people who hold such beliefs and who score high on one or more of the competences would usually report that they don't see subgroups in their teams, whereas people who see less value in diversity and are less competent in these areas, would report that they see subgroups in their teams. But this is not the pattern we found.

Instead, we found only one competence showing that precious relationship with subgroup perception. This competence is Managing Uncertainty. People scoring high on Managing Uncertainty report seeing fewer subgroups in their teams than people scoring low on Managing Uncertainty.[40] The relationship was highly significant, and strong enough to pass the generally accepted threshold that tells us that the effect we found is real.

This is an extraordinary finding. It suggests that one team member who can truly manage the uncertainty of intercultural interaction can make a real difference to a (culturally) diverse team, regardless of whether they are in a leading role.

Team members who are interculturally sensitive, competent intercultural communicators, able to build commitment, and who believe in diversity, do contribute to a diverse team's performance. But all alone, they are unlikely to escape from the crazy social dynamics that can take root in diverse teams. A person scoring high on Intercultural Sensitivity, Intercultural Communication or Building Commitment would still need the other team members to believe in diversity and be interculturally competent, so that they can jointly create a constructive team reality (without those nasty subgroups).

People scoring high on Managing Uncertainty, in contrast, can deal with the emotional and cognitive uncertainty that comes with differences. They enjoy the kick and the challenge associated with vagueness and ambiguity, having multiple options and turbulent team dynamics, and they don't feel anxious when the team is in disagreement and still open in all directions. Because high scorers on Managing Uncertainty suffer less from the anxiety and uncertainty that comes with diversity, they don't need to inappropriately reduce the anxiety through the comfort and safety of forming subgroups in which people look alike, don't need to process differences emotionally and intellectually, and can quickly agree on what should be thought and done. A person scoring high on Managing Uncertainty might actually be quite bored with a homogeneous subgroup or a homogeneous team.

For culturally diverse teams to succeed, they need to get a grip on their processes (see Box 6.7 for an case study example of successful leadership of a culturally divers team). First and foremost, they must avoid falling into subgroups. Positive diversity beliefs play a pivotal role: if the whole team believes in its diversity it will not perceive subgroups, despite objective risk, because no such subgroups have formed.

The IRC competences show clear and strong relationships to people's diversity beliefs, such that people with high scores on IRC competences usually also believe in the value that differences bring to their team. When all or most members of a team score high on the IRC, showing that they are highly interculturally competent, the team is very likely to successfully use its diversity as an asset for performance, outperforming homogeneous teams in terms of creativity, innovation and decision-making. Teams scoring high on Building Commitment and Managing Uncertainty will be especially likely to get things sorted. These teams will need only minimal external support, combined with a clearly spelled-out vision of just how their differences are needed for performance.

But all on their own, people with positive diversity beliefs and high scores on Intercultural Sensitivity, Intercultural Communication and Building Commitment are unlikely to prevent a team from falling into subgroups. They are just as likely to suffer from their team falling into subgroups as are people with less developed beliefs and competences in these areas. In contrast, a single person with high scores on Managing Uncertainty may substantially contribute to preventing the team from splitting up. This person may be the team leader or a regular team member, but if they score high on Managing Uncertainty, the difference they can make is truly unique.

BOX 6.7 CASE STUDY: LEADING A CULTURALLY DIVERSE TEAM

Adrian Degen* is General Manager of a company in the oil and gas extraction business, wholly owned by one of the largest corporations in Europe. We spoke to Adrian about his insights into achieving top performance in a culturally diverse team. Adrian spent four years in Argentina as General Manager of the company, and was faced with the task of creating a team that would be able to succeed in the extremely dynamic Argentine business environment.

Adrian has a strong multicultural background. Born and educated in Belgium, he is married to Beth, who works as an intercultural coach and trainer. Before he started to lead the company in Argentina, he and his family had already lived in England, the Netherlands and the Middle East; each of their three children was born in a different country. Adrian and his wife always wanted to live abroad; prepared for the local cultures, compared and analysed their intercultural encounters. Obviously, Adrian is not only a seasoned expatriate in terms of time served, but also well-versed in all matters cross cultural.

Oscar: 'Argentineans are famously paradoxical: sensitive to loss of face and lack of respect, yet very confrontational. Did you find that you had to use all your cultural fluency to steer through these conflicting demands?'

Adrian: 'In Argentina, people like to have a clash every now and then. What foreigners don't understand is that these don't resolve into win–win outcomes – everything has to do with loss of face, so someone has to win and someone has to lose. There were clashes when I felt uncomfortable – they seemed unethical, and clearly not in line with our company culture.'

Oscar: 'So this is the art of reconciling opposites: being determined and respectful at the same time?'

Adrian agrees: 'For me, open feedback has worked in Germany, the UK, the Netherlands, the Middle East and also in Argentina. Direct feedback, however, will be constructive only if your relationship is based on respect. This is independent of culture, period.'

Some Argentinean managers have been trained in a North American leadership style, which they take to mean being tough and pushing for results. But actually, this doesn't fit the local culture. You need to constantly fine-tune your approach, be alert to often contradictory demands. You need to follow your own approach without ever disrespecting the local culture.'

The business environment in Argentina is dynamic and complex, if only for the countless new tax regulations every year. And the oil and gas industry is particularly knotty. What happens here matters to the government – its natural resources are crucially important to the country's future. Hence, a company may be confronted with unforeseen demands that affect its agreements with other stakeholders, inside and outside Argentina.

Adrian comments dryly: 'Some fellow expatriates who went from Buenos Aires to Moscow say Russia is a stroll in the park.'

Adrian has an open, coaching-oriented leadership style, which contrasted with the more directive, results-oriented approach of his predecessor.

Adrian: 'My team was very diverse, consisting of Argentineans, Europeans and Asians. You need to really invest into building trust and inviting different perspectives. Otherwise, you focus only on people who are like you, you trust them intuitively to achieve the results, but you neglect building rapport with people who differ from you. Over time, this tends to drive a team apart, people no longer talk freely with each other.'

Oscar: 'Diversity in a team is problematic if it creates subgroups and cliques. Some people argue that to avoid subgroups, you should first have everyone focus on the task: setting clear guidelines for what needs to be done, and how you're going to work together. When that's done, then it's key to focus on the individuals, get to know their different perspectives. Is this how you started with your team?'

Adrian: 'You can focus on the task only if you first dedicate your time to each person individually. When I arrived, I first talked to each of my team members, for two or even three hours. I was interested in them personally, their background, their family; I asked them what made them proud to be Argentine. What were their ideas about moving forward, how to help people connect with each other again? From my managers, I wanted to know how they saw the situation, understand their image of the organization's future.'

When he felt that relationships were being established and re-built, Adrian formed small working groups around specific topics. He would still not use team meetings for discussions, but solely orchestrate them as information events. Relationships kept improving, people got along well with each other, and even invited each other to family events. In short, the team really stuck together.

Oscar: 'So what specifically told you that your approach was bearing fruit?'

Adrian: 'The key for me was when people started coming to me to tell me their opinion, but would then add, "Well, maybe you want to talk to him or her, they may have a different opinion." This for me was the signal that we really had become one team.'

Oscar: 'Before you had created that open team spirit, what had been your experience with taking decisions that could risk further polarizing a team?'

Adrian: 'I recall that in this process, I took one key decision at one stage, which was not to take a decision. We had two options about an important gas delivery contract, which involved choosing between two existing processing plants – where liquids are removed and dry gas and the liquids are sold separately. Each plant was advocated by a different key manager. Economically, the two options did not differ much from each other. However, the two key people differed in their assessment of the external conditions affecting our estimated profitability in the future: how much would our competitors produce in the two different regions where the processing plants are located? How would that affect our ability to accommodate all of our gas? This assessment, however, was difficult to verify, we had no hard facts on how their production would develop. The key managers had each committed to one of the plants, and factions had formed around them – even though economically the difference between the plants could not be quantified.

Since both approaches were equally valid, how could I make sure that the decision was objective? I had an internal consulting team fly in from Europe, I wanted them to analyse the two scenarios and give their advice. Since if whatever decision had just come from me, how could I be sure I was being impartial? And me being seen as taking sides would have forced people into one-sided loyalties, it would have caused a trench war, and I would not have been able to bring the team back together. When the consultants had spoken, the team started to relax.'

Oscar: 'About being in charge of an operation in a different culture, one often gets comments about the difficulties dealing with local authorities, could you share some of your experiences in this respect?'

Adrian: 'Yes, this often is a crucial issue that required a strong, creative team. At one stage, we faced demands from a regional government that affected our delivery contracts with partners outside Argentina. Basically, the government informed us that we were not allowed to deliver gas to certain clients of ours. But we had a legally binding contract with that client, and delivering the gas was absolutely vital for them – they had planned production around that delivery, and without our gas, they would have been forced to close their factories. So this would have had huge consequences for that client, and hence for us. With what we had on the table at that point in time, we would have lost – big time. It was one of those phone calls that leaves you shattered at your desk.

Subsequently, I probably made close to weekly trips to the client that year; and remember, we're not in a culture that believes in win–win. But we had formed a strong team by then and we refused to accept that a win–lose approach was our only option; within our management team we kept believing in win–win. My belief was nourished by the assessment within our team that one of the key people on our client's side was also ready to search for a win–win solution, which indeed he was.

This was not at all obvious initially, and in any case very hard work. One of our colleagues even quit because he could not see it happening. My whole team was in constant communication with their counterparts. Again, none of the usual agreements, ideas, solutions would have saved us. However, driven by the common goal across functional, professional, cultural, departmental and even company boundaries, people continued to communicate. In the end, our solution came jointly from our marketing people and the geologists – together with the client, we decided to invest jointly into a new area of business that would go far beyond the previous supplier–customer relationship. And I'm proud to say that we were the very first company in that situation coming up with such a solution.'

Oscar: 'Thank you very much Adrian, for this conversation.'

*The names of individuals have been changed to ensure confidentiality.

A Seven-Point Action Plan for Culturally Diverse Teams

Step 1. Assessing the Task Context: What is to Be Achieved, How and When?

People involved: this is usually the responsibility of line management and human resource management.

Given the output the team needs to achieve, assess how the team can benefit from differences. The more unusual, creative and innovative the solutions that are required, the more diversity can contribute to this.

Will the team members depend on each other's cooperation, or are there (open or hidden) incentives for team members to compete against each other for resources and rewards? If team members compete against each other, their differences will most likely affect them negatively.

How much time and other pressure do you anticipate for the team? How much support do you need to provide accordingly?

Will the team have the right degree of autonomy? If team members need to start by deciding on everything about the 'what, how, when and by whom' tasks must be done, they may quickly get lost in debates and conflicts before even starting to work together.

Step 2. Selection of Team Members: Who Should Be in the Team?

People involved: this is usually the responsibility of line management and human resource management.

In selecting team members, pay attention to the many ways in which people can differ, for example in gender, culture, ethnicity, language, age, company and professional background, seniority, tenure, personality, interaction and thinking styles.

If you have a choice, avoid creating a group that will easily fall into subgroups because multiple diversity features conspire. So avoid where possible creating a team with three female pilots in their thirties and three male psychologists in their fifties. Their differences can quickly conspire to create a strong faultline, with two homogeneous subgroups on either side, which may naturally hoard information and fight for power rather than cooperate.

If the team will be confronted with cultural differences, and if there is a risk that faultlines will develop, make sure you assess team members on their intercultural competences combined with confidential professional feedback. Use the team profile to determine how much support they will need from a professional intercultural facilitator.

Assess the team leader's leadership style. Does he or she have one dominant style – either always task-orientated or always relationship-orientated? To what extent is this leader able to switch between styles, and be a considerate/transformational leader? To what extent do they need coaching on leadership approach until the team is properly set up and working?

Step 3. Managing Communication, Reducing Conflict and Creating Cohesion

People involved: the team leader negotiating the 'what, how, when and with whom' with line management, human resource management and other key stakeholders in the organization will be the person involved here.

The nature of the task: assess how complex and demanding the task faced by your team is. If it is complex and demanding, your culturally diverse team may suffer more conflicts. You will need to pay extra attention to showing value in diversity and creating safety and clarity in your team.

Be clear about how the team's goals contribute to organizational goals, and push for all the resources you can get.

Who set the goals? If they were set by people who themselves differed from each other, for instance, in terms of their cultural background, double-check whether they invested enough effort into clarifying potentially different interpretations of these goals.

Push for flexibility on how you can assign roles. You do not know your team members well enough yet, so you may not know enough yet about the roles individuals can fulfil and grow in. Remember that team members must also be able to satisfy their personal needs and ambitions through the teamwork, and their roles must, to the extent possible, fit those needs.

The more you push for some leeway now, the better you can demonstrate to your team from the start that you carved out enough time for everyone to learn about their differences and how each can contribute in a unique way.

Assess your own intercultural competences, and request confidential feedback on the results from an intercultural professional who is external to your organization.

Reflect on your leadership style: do you give enough personal consideration and can you switch from a task-oriented to a relationship-oriented style?

Work out precisely how the team's diversity will be needed for performance. You must be able to state firmly the value of your team's diversity for achieving its performance goals – even if you're half asleep, have jetlag or can only use text messages for communicating with your team.

Step 4. Team Members Get to Know Each Other and Build Rapport

People involved: this is the particular responsibility of the team leader but also of team members.

Since your team is likely to be diverse, both culturally and in other ways, the team will need to invest extra effort into understanding each other before they can benefit from their diversity. Allocate enough time for this.

Make it clear that cultural differences exist in the team, and that these differences are welcome and needed. Remember that a 'colour-blind' attitude will not get your team one step further.

Address explicitly the fact that more time is needed for mutual understanding and trust, in order for you all to perform at your best later on. This will help the more task-driven members of your team to be patient.

Appoint an external team facilitator to help your team deal with its greater processing and communicating demands, at least in the early phases of the task.

Familiarize yourself with facilitation techniques so that you can balance interaction and contributions of all members. A simple example is to structure discussion in a 'round robin' style, so that everyone contributes, one after another. Another option is to initiate ten-minute silent brainstorming during which people write up their ideas on cards, which others can read. After the ten minutes, cluster the cards into meaningful groups and give each team member (including yourself) five votes to rate how important/urgent/useful the clusters are.

Encourage your team members to assess their intercultural competences, and combine this with confidential feedback from an intercultural professional. If you are using the IRC, ask for an IRC group profile to see how high your team scores on all competences, and especially how many people score high on Managing Uncertainty. These may be your best allies in avoiding the formation of subgroups.

Step 5. Process and Performance Responsibility

People involved: this is an individual responsibility of both the team manager and individual team members.

Invest extra time into individual conversations between team leader and team members. In each case, double-check whether you both understand the team's task in the same way, and listen for cues indicating different interpretations.

As a team member, clarify your personal needs, obligations and goals. Help your team leader to understand what is important to you – they are not psychic!

Ask yourself what is your unique contribution to the team. Which extra ideas, perspective and contacts can you bring in?

Which relationships in the team are already strong, which ones need to be strengthened so that you can envision working with everyone again on another project?

Reflect upon how you can use the teamwork to bring in your intercultural competences, and enhance these.

People involved: team responsibility – team manager and team members.

Use facilitation techniques to balance interaction and contributions of all members.

Be aware that people in your team may have different ideas about the role of the team leader, and those of the other team members. What are your ideas about a good leader? Imagine alternative ideas.

Carefully attend to verbal and nonverbal cues suggesting misunderstandings, then explore these misunderstandings to better learn about each other, and to get to know the different perspectives that your team will benefit from later.

Always be pro-diversity and do not allow faultlines to develop and fester.

Mix and vary who works with whom. Work with people who differ from you – have a gender-mixed group today, a culture-mixed group tomorrow.

Vary the number of people working together. Working in pairs helps us to understand each other at a more personal level, and will allow you to address emotional topics. Use groups of three if you need a devil's advocate to avoid premature consensus. With more than four people working together, make sure you involve everyone to contribute to discussions, for example, through a round robin, turn-taking exercise.

In complex face-to-face discussions, and for a range of team interactions taking place across distances, engage one person to moderate the interaction – ideally the one who is least involved with the content of the discussion but who understands what is being discussed.

Make regular checks on team performance. Assess both task-related output and team members' ability to work together again, and, as the team feels more comfortable with each other, also address the need to have one's personal interests and goals satisfied through the teamwork.

Celebrate your success.

Step 6. Feedback on Process and Results

People involved: the human resource manager, line manager and team.

Assess all three team performance criteria: task-related output, ability to work together again and satisfaction of personal needs and goals.

Evaluate how both the social-emotional process and the informational process have been working.

Reflect on how the team's diversity has benefited the team so that you continue to foster pro-diversity beliefs.

Show your success.

Step 7. Learning for Future Teams

People involved: learning and development and human resource management perspective.

How does the team's success contribute to your organization's attitude towards diversity?

What can your organization learn from the team's success, and how can it integrate the different perspectives that were expressed and evolved?

What do key stakeholders need to learn about each team member's unique contribution? Ensure that nobody is overlooked.

7

What Makes an Organization Interculturally Competent?

One final, important finding comes from a cross-comparison of IRC scores: that diversity management is key to intercultural readiness of organizations.

One specific result is surprising in how clear and wide-ranging is its effect: organizations in which women are well represented at top management levels are more interculturally competent than those who lack women in these positions. But it is not just that women in key positions raise the competence levels of the organization. Staff at all levels – men and women alike – are more interculturally competent in organizations with more women in top functions.

This may be, we think, because diversity is a core value for many women. Diversity management only works if an organization is willing to change, and to learn from the perspectives of all its members. Women are particularly willing to drive this change. A comparison of men's and women's beliefs in diversity, using our databank of their answers to the IRC questions, shows that women are stronger defenders of diversity than men.

Effective diversity management pays off: it makes the entire organization interculturally more competent and it brings diversity's strongest defenders into key positions – to the benefit of all teams and all people in the organization.

Enabling Intercultural Competences

Our research has found that organizations can enable staff to be interculturally competent, through fostering a value deeply ingrained in their way of functioning – part of their reproductive DNA – so that all employees are continually encouraged to develop their intercultural competences. How such a value can be instilled is illustrated in Box 7.1.

Such an organization will have many culturally competent people – not because only culturally competent people are ever hired, but because the organization has *enabled* its people to continually develop these competences.

BOX 7.1 DEALING WITH STATUS ISSUES

An example of an organization that demonstrated deep commitment to its belief in diversity, when this value was put under pressure in a cross-border negotiation, was a European multinational that had started negotiations with a Japanese supplier back in the 1990s. As head of the negotiation team they had appointed a woman – a high-profile lawyer with years of experience in her field. By all accounts she was the right person for this job. But after a week in Japan, negotiations were not progressing.

The lawyer explained to her bosses in Europe that she had reason to believe that this particular negotiation team, whose members were all male, were uncomfortable negotiating with a woman. The Japanese team, she said, did not necessarily doubt her abilities, but she correctly deduced that they were concerned about how they would be perceived if seen to be negotiating with a woman, whose status had not been made clear to them. So they were stalling the negotiation.

For the European multinational, clearly the value of supporting a diverse workforce was in conflict with the opportunity to do business. Its executives were keenly aware that replacing their lead negotiator with a man would call into doubt their commitment to diversity. So they looked for other options – and found a clever solution.

Apparently their female negotiator needed more status in the eyes of this particular Japanese team. So the company arranged for her to give a lecture at the prestigious Tokyo University, and invited her negotiation partners to attend. They also arranged for their lawyer and the Japanese team to be invited to a high-profile dinner at their national embassy in Tokyo, where they were seated together.

Soon after, the negotiations started again. Now the Japanese negotiation team felt assured that the choice of a female lead negotiator was not meant to be disrespectful. And there was a positive side effect: as a result of the successful negotiations, this woman became a role-model for female corporate executives in the Asia Pacific region, and the Japanese executives were honoured to deal with this high-status lawyer.

Working with very different organizations, and assessing the intercultural competences of their staff, we were struck by how confidently some companies dealt with their intercultural challenges, and how much others still struggled. Were these just accidental observations, or did people differ indeed in cultural competence levels depending on the organization they worked for? To find out, we first tested whether some organizations have more interculturally competent staff than others, and if so, whether the organization's commitment to diversity could explain the results. This was the goal of an analysis of the IRC database conducted by psychologist Annemarie Kohne.

Benchmarking Organizations for Intercultural Competences

In 2008, Annemarie Kohne, then an MA student of psychology at the University of Amsterdam, analysed the IRC database to test whether IRC competence levels would differ between organizations. The research was the basis of her MA thesis, 'An Analysis of Differences in Intercultural Competences between Industries', supervised by psychologists Dr Ursula Brinkmann (co-author of the book) and Dr Dianne van Hemert.[1]

At that time, 8601 people had filled in the IRC, and for most of these it was possible to determine the company they worked for, and in turn the corresponding industry (for example, Shipping or Investment Banking) and sector to which the companies belonged (for example, Transportation or Finance and Insurance).[2] For ten sectors, more than 100 respondents from different management levels had submitted their data to the IRC, leaving a total of 6583 respondents. The sectors and the number of respondents per sector are shown in Table 7.1.

After classifying companies into sectors, we calculated the average IRC scores of respondents working in a given sector, to measure their

Table 7.1 Industry sectors and respondents per sector in the IRC benchmarking study

Industry sector	Number of IRC respondents per sector
Administrative Services	148
Educational Services	747
Finance and Insurance	1858
Food, Beverage, Tobacco and Textile Manufacturing	153
Metal Manufacturing (for example, manufacture of machinery, automotive, computer and electronics)	964
Non-metal Manufacturing (for example, chemical and pharmaceutical manufacturing)	1013
Professional, Scientific and Technical Services	218
Public Administration	249
Retail Trade	268
Transportation	965
Total	6583

intercultural competences as a group. Would the sectors differ in terms of the average IRC scores of people working in that sector?

They did indeed. For all four IRC competences, the differences between the sectors in terms of IRC average scores were highly significant.

To find out which sectors scored highest and which lowest on intercultural competences, we compared the sectors as pairs, comparing each sector against each of the other nine sectors. This time, clear differences were found for three IRC competences: Intercultural Communication, Building Commitment and Managing Uncertainty. The Public Administration sector scored particularly high on Intercultural Communication, outperforming all other sectors except Administrative Services.

Administrative Services itself scored high on Intercultural Communication, outperforming Educational Services, Retail Trade and Transportation, as well as Finance and Insurance. For the intercultural competence Building Commitment – that competence so characteristic of senior executives – Transportation scored lower than Metal Manufacturing; and for Managing Uncertainty, Transportation scored lower than both Metal Manufacturing and Finance and Insurance. What could explain these differences in competence levels?

Effective Diversity Management

We were particularly interested in whether diversity management would contribute to the intercultural competences of its employees. With an increasingly diverse workforce, companies need to manage their diversity – that is, they need to find a way of 'enabling every member of [the] work force to perform to his or her potential', as R. Roosevelt Thomas Jr, in his article, 'From Affirmative Action to Affirming Diversity', succinctly defines it.[3]

Many organizations struggle to make their diversity initiatives work. Despite numerous efforts, dedicated projects and substantial budgets, staff from non-dominant groups (for example, women and members of ethnic minority groups) are kept as if by force of gravity at the bottom of the organizational hierarchy.

We use the metaphor 'force of gravity' to indicate that it is always a range of factors – the hidden power of stereotypes, the 'similarity attracts' principle, the importance of role models, criteria for performance heavily influenced by the dominant culture, to name just a few – that organizations have to manage if they want to enable all members to perform to their potential. How difficult this can be is illustrated in Box 7.2.

BOX 7.2 WHO'S OF THE RIGHT STUFF?[4]

A study by psychologists Anneke M. Sools and Marloes L. van Engen and sociologist Chris Baerveldt, 'Gendered Career-Making Practices: on "Doing Ambition" or How Managers Discursively Position Themselves in a Multinational Corporation', describes how women were put at a disadvantage in a Dutch multinational through taboos around career ambition in combination with implicit evaluation processes.

In this company, it was not done to openly admit one's ambition for promotion. When asked about future goals, the code was to stress one's desire to be challenged by new projects. But this ambition was not assessed through regular performance reviews or formal evaluation procedures designed to properly determine a candidate's suitability for promotion. Instead, one just had to demonstrate one's ambition through hard work and extra hours, and to convince decision-makers that one would stay equally ambitious and committed for years to come. In addition, decision-makers believed they could identify who was 'made of the right stuff' by simply observing people and going on their resulting gut feeling.

The secrecy about career ambition, and the way in which decision-makers selected people, put women at a disadvantage – women in their thirties were expected to get pregnant sooner or later and to work part-time after the child was born, which in practice would put them off the career track. Women who were ambitious and fully committed to their careers, with or without children, could not convince their bosses of their determination – because of the company's code, they could neither talk openly about their career ambition, nor convince their bosses that they would not start to work part-time work once they had had their first child.

Just how effectively that force of gravity is keeping members of non-dominant groups at the lower levels of the organizational hierarchy, is confirmed by our own data, which we collected from 2001 to 2013. Table 7.2 shows, for 29,650 people who answered the IRC, the proportion of men and women at different management levels. Across hundreds of organizations from all over the world, the higher we get in the organization, the fewer women we see, a finding that echoes the results of numerous reports on gender diversity management in organizations.

Among people without management responsibility (respondents who said they have no people reporting directly to them), men and women are almost equally represented in the database (with 52 per cent men and 48 per cent women). But with every step in management level, the proportion tips towards there being more men than women, and at the highest level of management, where respondents have 50 or more people directly reporting to them, 83 per cent of respondents are men, and just 17 per cent women.

In 29,650 IRC reports, the picture of women's place in organizations is starkly evident. From an almost equal number of men and women among those with no one reporting to them, the figures gradually skew to the point where almost nine in ten of those with more than 50 people reporting to them are male.

Table 7.2   Proportion of men and women by management level

Given that so many organizations struggle to make their diversity initiatives work, we were particularly interested in those organizations whose initiatives had shown effect. Would their commitment to diversity translate into higher intercultural competences of their staff?

To test for a link between diversity management and intercultural competences, we focused on *gender diversity management*, that is, the degree to which women and men are represented equally at all levels of an organization's hierarchy. Would the ten sectors of our benchmarking study differ in their competence levels depending on how many women within a company held senior management positions?

We considered positions where managers had 11 or more people directly reporting to them to be senior management positions, and ranked the companies in our database depending on how many women were in senior management positions.

The correlation between companies having women at the top and being strong in intercultural competences came out clearly: the higher the percentage of women in top leadership positions throughout a sector, the higher the sector's overall IRC competence scores.

This result was confirmed in an additional analysis, in which we used a cut-off point of companies having 30 per cent or more women in top positions. This is considerably above the average percentage of women in top positions, shown in Table 7.2, which is 24 per cent for women with 11 to 50 people directly reporting to them, and 17 per cent for women with more than 50 direct reports.

Only one of the ten sectors met the 30 per cent criterion: Administrative Services. For this calculation, the IRC competence scores of the sector Administrative Services were compared against the IRC competence scores of all the other nine sectors taken together. As expected, Administrative Services scored significantly higher on Intercultural Sensitivity, Intercultural Communication and Building Commitment than all other sectors.

Importantly, in both analyses, it was not just the female top executives who had better competence scores. In that case, it might be argued that the women in these positions, having overcome so many obstacles, were particularly culturally competent, and so with more women in senior management positions, the top overall scored better. Instead, across *all management levels*, and for men and women alike, the average IRC competence scores per sector were higher the more women held top management functions in a sector. Effective gender diversity management enables both male and female staff to develop their intercultural competences.

Our benchmarking study shows that diversity management and intercultural competences are connected. When an organization succeeds in enabling all employees to perform to their potential, it may enjoy a highly desirable extra benefit: people working for this organization will be interculturally more competent than people working for other organizations.

But effective diversity management can have another unexpected benefit, as an analysis of men's and women's belief in diversity shows.

Promoting the Strongest Defenders of Diversity

In Chapter 6, we discussed how people's beliefs in diversity and their intercultural competences are connected. Thousands of people had told us about what they thought about the value of diversity for their teams. As expected, we found that people who are convinced that diversity has value for their teams also had strongly developed intercultural competences.

In analysing the answers of 4390 people who had filled in the IRC and told us about their diversity beliefs, we conducted one additional statistical test. We wanted to know whether women, as likely members of a non-dominant group in the workplace, would feel stronger about the value of diversity for their teams than men, who are more likely to represent the dominant group in the workplace.

BOX 7.3 SCOPE OF OUR STUDY

Women in organizations are a special case as members of non-dominant groups, and what holds for their assumptions about diversity may not hold for other non-dominant groups.

First, women are not members of a *minority* group in society, whereas diversity in terms of ethnicity, for example, often implies that there is an ethnic majority and one or more ethnic minorities outside the organization.

Second, those women who come from the dominant ethnic group in their country are not seen as potentially threatening the country's traditional cultural values and norms, as is often the case with immigrant groups, and so they are not prone to the specific negative stereotypes that may result from that sense of threat.

Women also come from all groups in a society, from low-status groups to high-status groups. Coming from an ethnic minority, in contrast, may go in tandem with a lower socioeconomic status and on average less access to higher education.

In many countries, women by now achieve the same levels of education as men, and they often enjoy the fruits of decades of feminism, which has stressed their equal rights to higher education and organizational positions.

Women's sense of self and their experiences as members of a non-dominant group may thus differ considerably from the sense of self and the experiences that members of ethnic minority groups in a society may have. Therefore, our findings apply only for women in the context of gender diversity; they may or may not hold for other non-dominant groups.

Why would we expect women to be more positive about diversity in their teams than men? For one thing, women are more likely than men to bring diversity to the workplace, just by being women. Men and women are not equally represented at all levels of hierarchy in an organization. This means that the higher the management level at which women operate, the more diversity they bring to their team.

Because they themselves bring diversity to their team, women should be more likely than their male colleagues to value their team's diversity – if only because of the self-serving bias that makes so many of us feel actually quite good about ourselves.

Men, in contrast, while often strongly committed to diversity in general and to gender diversity in particular, are more likely to work in a male-only team, where gender diversity is not a topic. And even if their team consists of both men and women, male team members may often not see themselves as belonging to a particular group with its own cultural ways, and so may not see that they bring their own diversity to the group. As is so often the case, members of dominant groups in an organization or society find it hardest to see what makes them special, because the world around them is designed so that they don't have to bother with being special. Think of right-handed people, who do not see that scissors, brooms, guitars, faucets and circular saws are designed just for them. It is the left-handed ones among us who are constantly confronted with a world that doesn't work.

We were interested in the views of women for a very specific reason. If women indeed valued diversity in their teams higher than men, this would be good news: it would suggest that by developing and promoting members of non-dominant groups, organizations might be able to seize upon an unexpected benefit – people would get into key positions who are deeply convinced of the value diversity brings to their team and organization. And through seeing value in diversity, these managers in turn would help their teams to perform and benefit from their diversity.

Of the respondents who had expressed their diversity beliefs on the IRC databank we were studying, 2632 were men and 1758 were women. Both groups highly value diversity for their teams: on a scale from a minimum of 4 (seeing no value in diversity) and a maximum of 28 points (being fully convinced of diversity's value), women on average give 25.26 points and men give 24.25 points. So both men and women see value in diversity and support it.

But even though these group averages differ by just a single point, that difference is significant: female respondents value diversity in their teams significantly more than men do, and they do so consistently across all levels of management. Male respondents, in contrast, value diversity depending on their level in the management hierarchy: those who have no or initial management responsibility value diversity less than those with senior management responsibility (see Table 7.3).

Table 7.3   Diversity beliefs by gender depending on management level

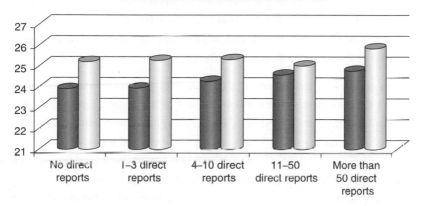

Table 7.3 shows the scores for diversity beliefs for men and women depending on management level, with higher scores indicating more positive diversity beliefs (from those with no others reporting to them to those with more than 50 people reporting to them). While both groups value diversity, female respondents value diversity in their teams more than male respondents, and more consistently so across management levels. Male respondents with no or initial management responsibility see less value in diversity than male respondents who have more management responsibility.

Effective Diversity Management Enables Intercultural Readiness

Our findings show that effective diversity management pays off: it makes the entire organization more interculturally competent and it brings diversity's strongest defenders into key positions – to the benefit of all teams and all people in the organization. Effective diversity management enables intercultural readiness, which in turn makes the entire organization more interculturally effective.

Effective diversity management gets an organization into a virtuous self-reinforcing loop of learning and development. Through the promotion of staff from non-dominant groups, strong defenders of diversity get into key positions. Their power to positively influence the organization increases. They can support their diverse teams to see value in diversity and so to benefit from their differences and achieve superior results. The members of these teams in turn will successfully manage their own diverse teams.

Across all levels of management, people working in teams learn from each other's different perspectives and so achieve better results. Everyone in the organization experiences first-hand that diversity brings benefits. Working in successful diverse teams, backed by an organization that is deeply committed to diversity, all members of the organization are enabled to develop their intercultural competence potential. Developing this potential, which we call intercultural readiness, will in turn make everyone interculturally effective when interacting with customers, colleagues and other stakeholders from different groups, and from different cultures and countries.

Perspectives on Diversity – Diversity as a Source of Learning and Integration

Intercultural readiness requires people, teams and organizations to be open to change, and to actively seek information about what needs changing. Change requires more than adding new information to existing knowledge. It means being open to reconsider what one has taken for granted, if new information suggests this is necessary. Other cultures help us to discover what we've been taking for granted, and to imagine alternatives.

Studies on diversity management show how people can be willing to change, only to get all tangled up in a sticky web of good intentions and ill-understood, unforeseen consequences.

How such sticky webs can keep people and organizations from turning good intentions into better realities in the absence of change is captured by Professors of Business Administration Robin J. Ely and David A. Thomas in their landmark study, 'Cultural Diversity at Work: The Effects of Diversity Perspectives on Work Group Processes and Outcomes'.[5]

Ely and Thomas studied three US organizations, which differed in what the authors call their 'diversity perspectives' – that is, the 'group members' normative beliefs and expectations about cultural diversity and its role in their work group' (p. 234). Only one of these perspectives worked, while the other two perspectives had unforeseen and wickedly negative effects on employees' ability to deal with their cultural differences.

The diversity perspective that worked was a perspective in which differences between ethnic groups were seen as a resource for learning and integration, and as a *legitimate reason for change*.

The **Learning and Integration** perspective of diversity is marked by four features:

1. The organization opens itself to people from non-dominant groups in its society in order to reflect on and improve its core work goals and work processes.
2. People's cultural identity, their position in society in terms of recognition and power, and their life experiences, are used as a resource for learning and for redefining the organization. Cultural differences are seen as a potential source of information for learning about and re-evaluating the organization's goals and processes.
3. Cultural diversity and the work people do are understood as intrinsically connected. People from different cultural groups are not just added on, having to adapt to existing processes and goals, but bring in new perspectives about what to do, and how to do it.
4. Progress in managing diversity is measured through giving people from traditionally under-represented groups a voice, and giving them the power to change the organization; at the same time, members of traditionally dominant groups are willing to change. Change can affect the process of working and can lead to new products and services.

Everyone's commitment to change implies a shared view of cultural diversity as a resource for learning and integration.

The two ineffective diversity perspectives, with their unforeseen negative dynamics, were the **Access and Legitimacy** perspective and the **Discrimination and Fairness** perspective, which are described in more detail in Box 7.4.

Ely and Thomas show that *only the Learning and Integration perspective of diversity works*, while the Access and Legitimacy perspective and the Discrimination and Fairness perspective have an unexpected built-in negative dynamic, and so should not be adopted.

To effectively manage their diversity, organizations need to define how and why differences contribute to performance. Without such a vision, cultural differences, or group differences of any other kind, remain a nuisance to efficiency. Based on such a vision, however, organizations can start to create a self-reinforcing loop of learning and development that will enable all of its members to develop their intercultural readiness.

BOX 7.4 DIVERSITY PERSPECTIVES THAT DO NOT WORK[6]

The Access and Legitimacy perspective was found in a company that had hired African American staff to access a special market segment – customers with a predominantly African American working-class background. This market was less important and prestigious than the company's other markets, which mainly served wealthy white customers. The new market remained a marginal activity.

African American staff serving these customers lacked power inside the organization and so had to adapt to its existing goals and processes. They were successful if they generated profit, but were not seen as colleagues bringing unique perspectives and skills that others could learn from. Since the differences between groups inside the organization mirrored the status and power differences in the overall society, conflicts between people were difficult and emotionally loaded. The members of the non-dominant group did not have the power to change, nor were the members of the dominant group willing or called upon to change.

But it was the Discrimination and Fairness perspective that had the most pernicious effects. The company where Ely and Thomas identified this approach to diversity had hired people from different ethnic backgrounds in order to do the right thing. There was no specific business reason for diversifying that would have provided a measure for performance. In the absence of such measures, people became anxious to avoid at all costs doing anything that might be seen as discriminatory and unfair.

Members of the dominant group became afraid to say anything critical to their colleagues, or give feedback on work and performance. But without feedback, staff from the non-dominant groups felt not valued as colleagues who wanted to invest in their professionalism, and were excluded from the organizational learning curve.

The very reason for hiring people from non-dominant groups – their special cultural membership – had turned into a taboo topic. People kept their frustrations to themselves, tiptoeing around each other. Any discussion of different cultural perspectives was quickly seen as discrimination, and sensitive topics like real and existing power differences could not be addressed.

Ironically, it was the Discrimination and Fairness perspective that led people to behave as if they were 'colour-blind', as if they did not differ in terms of culture and life experiences. Locked up inside their ethnic groups, people from the non-dominant groups felt frustrated and powerless, while those from the dominant group felt frustrated and apprehensive.

Key Points

- Effective diversity management enables people to develop their intercultural competences.
- Organizations in which women are well-represented in top positions foster intercultural competence development: they have more culturally competent men and women at all levels in the organization than those that lack women in top positions.
- Women are stronger defenders of diversity than men. By promoting women, organizations bring the strongest advocates of diversity into key positions.
- Effective diversity management means that diversity is recognized for what it is: an opportunity for continuous learning. But people from all groups must be enabled to change core organizational processes and goals, and key decision-makers must be willing to change.
- Effective diversity management creates a self-reinforcing loop of learning and development. Promoting staff from non-dominant groups brings the strongest defenders of diversity into key positions from which they can support diverse teams to benefit from their differences. Working in successful diverse teams, backed by an organization that is deeply committed to diversity, all members of an organization will become interculturally more effective both inside and outside the organization because they are enabled to continually develop their intercultural readiness.

A case study example of an organization that has successfully made diversity and inclusiveness a central value is given in Box 7.5.

BOX 7.5 CASE STUDY: FOSTERING INCLUSIVENESS

Dominique Fournier, Senior Consultant and Board Member of Kraton Performance Polymers, Inc.

As CEO of the US/British multinational Infinium from 2005 to 2011, Dominique Fournier determined that the company would make diversity and inclusiveness a central value. Infinium is the company that makes our cars run cleaner and last longer: it makes the additives that improve gasoline performance in automobiles, boats, trucks and machinery. The 80-year-old company has a presence on three continents, worldwide production facilities and business conducted in 20 languages.

'Our strategy had three components: commercial excellence, technology excellence and organizational excellence,' says Mr Fournier. 'We targeted advantage capabilities where we wanted to be much better than anybody else.'

One of the main targets was 'diversity and inclusiveness'. As an organization-wide value, this was mandated for all executives, and the results were tested every six months. Women and non-English-speakers were deliberately brought into the most senior decision-making levels of the company, and diversity and inclusiveness added to the official target list of executives.

For six years Infinium tracked the effects of this policy, and the results were astonishing. It had completely changed the culture of the company. Voluntary surveys were answered by 80 per cent of staff, and of these, 75 per cent said they were happy to work for Infinium, and ready to recommend to their friends and their children that they should go to work there. 'When you recommend to your son or daughter to work for a company, it's a sign that you're very happy with that company,' says Mr Fournier.

Diversity is difficult, he says: 'And it's not just Anglo-Saxons: the Japanese, and many other people I know from other cultures, are just as anti-diverse. It's much more comfortable to work with people like yourself, much more reinforcing and reassuring. Being always with people who you're not sure what they're really thinking, who keep you on your toes all the time, is extremely painful and stressing.'

But if you work hard to make a team of diverse cultures into a cooperative, happy group, there are huge benefits. If you have diversity, you avoid the danger of groupthink. Mr Fournier illustrates the dangers of groupthink with the story of a mono-cultural group who travelled to Singapore to look at building a factory there.

They came back gloomy. 'This won't fly with the management,' they said. 'We would be better to recommend expanding a French factory rather than building a new factory within the Asian base.' They had convinced each other, because they all thought alike. They had group thought themselves into agreement.

But they were wrong. Their top managers, who were now committed to an approach valuing diversity, looked at the figures and – even though the Singapore factory was going to cost 50 per cent more to run – overruled their decision. It was more important for the Asian market to have a local producer, a local footprint, a local presence.

A Short Checklist: What is the Perspective on Diversity in Your Organization?

Look around you in meetings, when you walk along the hallway, in the canteen. How many people do you see who come from non-dominant groups in your society? Does the mix reflect the composition of groups in your society?

When people apply for jobs in your company, how many applicants come from non-dominant groups in your society? You may not be attracting all the talent that is out there.

At an assessment conference a few years ago, we had a lively debate about how difficult it is to fairly and appropriately assess people from different groups within a society. We noticed the eyes of one participant glazing over. When we asked what was wrong, he replied, 'Well, we just don't seem to have that problem. We don't get any applicants from other ethnic groups'. He was the HR manager of an insurance firm in one of the most ethnically diverse cities in all of Europe.

If your company has invested in hiring people from non-dominant groups, what has been the rationale for hiring them? Was their membership of these groups part of the reason for hiring them? If so, how can these people contribute to your organization? Is the benefit they can bring mainly defined – and for all the good reasons – as accessing new market segments and for the purpose of gaining legitimacy with other customer groups? Is it to fight against discrimination and for fairness? These are important goals – but they may keep your organization from getting to where it wants to be.

Which ideas have been formulated for how staff from dominant and non-dominant groups could learn from each other? Observe and listen: do you pick up signals that learning is – consciously or unconsciously – defined as a one-way street? How could your organization's goals and processes be updated, sharpened, revised, revolutionized through insights from members of non-dominant groups?

Which situations have been created in which people can spend quality time for an exchange about their personal backgrounds, with no external pressure to achieve results, and a structure for dialogue – possibly with the help of a neutral but informed moderator – so that everybody can speak and feel they are listened to? Imagine a female employee who just got married and will now live with her in-laws from Pakistan. In Pakistan, a key decision-maker for a woman's career is her mother-in-law: she needs to back the wife's choice to continue working. Time spent in dialogue is needed to find out about such hidden constraints, and to explore how they can be addressed.

What are the organizational channels through which the outcomes of such conversations will be fed back to decision-makers? How do these decision-makers demonstrate that they have taken the new ideas and thoughts into account, and that they are willing to change?

How normal would it be to have a spontaneous conversation with a colleague from a different ethnic group about your potentially different life experiences? Would one or both of you feel awkward, or uncertain about what to say? If you come from the dominant group in your society, or in your organization, how comfortable would you find it to speak openly about your group's privileged status?

In using the IRC with ethnic minority groups in the Netherlands, we have noticed that some respondents score relatively low on Intercultural

Sensitivity. When we address this, they usually say that they don't feel comfortable talking about their cultural background with colleagues – either both parties pretend there is no difference in background, or else they themselves have been confronted with cultural stereotypes too often. As a result, they never felt motivated to understand their two cultural backgrounds – that of the dominant Dutch culture and that of their particular ethnic group – and so they never developed their Intercultural Sensitivity.

How accepted and common is it to have difficult conversations, or even conflict, and to know that such conversations are needed and will turn out well if conducted with empathy and with the taking seriously of each other's differing needs?

Are you confident and happy that your organization is benefiting from the best in intercultural readiness? Could it be better?

Diversity Perspective in My Organization

a) Using a subjective scale from 1 to 10, tick on the scales below where you see your organization's perspective on diversity (with 1 = not at all characteristic of my organization and 10 = very characteristic of my organization).

Learning and Integration: 1 _____ 10

Access and Legitimacy: 1 _____ 10

Discrimination and Fairness: 1 _____ 10

b) Teamwork: get together with some colleagues to discuss the above points. Sit around a table with cards for taking notes and spend ten minutes brainstorming silently on the following question:

What are some steps we could take to advance the Learning and Integration perspective in our organization?

During the brainstorming, jot down all ideas on separate cards and put them in the middle of the table for others to read.

After the brainstorming, cluster the cards and have everyone assign a total of five points to the clusters they find most relevant for action.

c) Decide which key people in your organization you need to get involved. How will you involve them? Which results would you want to see:

- after three months: _____

_____

- after six months: _____

_____

- after nine months: _____

_____

- after one year: _____

_____

- after two years: _____

_____

d) What will each of you commit to doing?

Stay Connected

Do you want to find out more about Intercultural Readiness, our network of IRC Licensees and exchanges on up-to-date topics? For resources, research findings and case studies, please visit http://www.irc-center.com and sign up to stay in touch through LinkedIn, Twitter and Email.

Notes

Introduction

1. Wade Davis is an anthropologist and biologist who works as explorer-in-residence for the National Geographic Society. He is author of numerous books, including the 1985 bestseller, *The Serpent and the Rainbow* (New York, NY: Touchstone), in which he investigates Haitian voodoo culture. For his plea to protect cultural diversity, see Wade Davis (2003) *Endangered Cultures*, TED talk presentation (http://www.ted.com/talks/wade_davis_on_endangered_cultures. Filed February 2003, posted January 2007. Retrieved 1 October 2013)

2. See Ursula Brinkmann and Oscar van Weerdenburg (2002) 'Risikomanagement bei der interkulturellen Zusammenarbeit', in Herbert J. Joka (ed.) *Führungskräftehandbuch* (Berlin, Germany: Springer) pp. 453–68; Karen I. van der Zee and Ursula Brinkmann (2004) 'Construct Validity Evidence for the Intercultural Readiness Check against the Multicultural Personality Questionnaire', *International Journal of Selection and Assessment,* Volume 12(3), pp. 285–90; Brinkmann and van Weerdenburg (2004) 'Training in Culturele Verschillen. Van Stereotiepe Beelden naar Interculturele Vaardigheden', *Management Tools,* Volume 3, pp. 24–9; and van Weerdenburg and Brinkmann (2011) 'Business Across Borders – No More Stumbling About', *IHRIM Publications, Workforce Solutions Review,* March–April issue (http://www.ihrimpublications.com/WSR_about.php)

3. All IRC scales are internally consistent. For Intercultural Sensitivity (10 items), alpha is 0.73; for Intercultural Communication (13 items), alpha is 0.82; for Building Commitment (20 items), it is 0.87, and for Managing Uncertainty (14 items) it is 0.78.

4. The scales we used in addition to the scales of the Intercultural Readiness Check come from the following sources:

   - The International Orientation scale was developed by Karen I. van der Zee; see, for example, van der Zee and Brinkmann (2004).

- Diversity beliefs: Astrid C. Homan, Lindred L. Greer, Karen A. Jehn and Lukas Koning (2010) 'Believing Shapes Seeing: The Impact of Diversity Beliefs on the Construal of Group Composition', *Group Processes & Intergroup Relations*, 13(4), pp. 477–93.
- Subgroup perception: Elaine L. Zanutto, Katerina Bezrukova and Karen A. Jehn (2011) 'Revisiting Faultline Conceptualization: Measuring Faultline Strength and Distance', *Quality & Quantity*, 45(3), pp. 701–14.

We are grateful to these researchers for allowing us to use the scales in our research.

Chapter 1: Intercultural Readiness: Turning Talent into Competence

1. Numbers from the following sources:

   - US Export fact sheet (April 2013) http://www.trade.gov/press/press-releases/2013/export-factsheet-april2013-040513.pdf.
   - Joachim Wagner (2012) 'Neue Fakten über Exporteure und Importeure. Eine Auswertung von Transaktionsdaten für 2009', *Wirtschaftsdienst. Zeitschrift für Wirtschaftspolitik*, Volume 92(7), pp. 496–8.
   - Union of International Associations (2011) *Yearbook of International Organizations 2011–2012. A Guide to Global Civil Society Networks. Volume 5: Statistics, visualizations and patterns*, pp. 33–5.

2. Numbers from the following sources:

   - Global Education Digest (2009) *Comparing Education Statistics Across the World* (UNESCO Institute for Statistics).
   - Website of the National University of Singapore (http://www.nus.edu.sg).
   - US Census Bureau (May 2012) *The Foreign-Born Population in the United States: 2010* (http://www.census.gov).
   - Jean-Christophe Dumont and Georges Lemaître (2008) 'Counting Foreign-Born and Expatriates in OECD Countries: A New Perspective', in James Raymer and Frans Willekens (eds) *International Migration in Europe: Data, Models and Estimates* (Chichester, UK: John Wiley & Sons) pp. 11–40.
   - United Arab Emirates National Bureau of Statistics (March 2011) *Population Estimates 2006–2010* (http://www.uaestatistics.gov.ae).
   - Kuwait Government Online: *Population of Kuwait* (http://www.e.gov.kw).

3. For an overview of research on how intercultural competences contribute to intercultural effectiveness, see David C. Thomas and Stacey R. Fitzsimmons (2008)

'Cross-Cultural skills and Abilities', in Peter B. Smith and Mark F. Peterson (eds) *The Handbook of Cross-Cultural Management Research* (London: SAGE) pp. 201–15.

4. See, for example, Brian F. Blake and Richard Heslin (1983) 'Evaluating Cross-Cultural training', in Dan Landis and Richard W. Brislin (eds) *Handbook of Intercultural Training* (New York: Pergamon); and Thomas and Fitzsimmons (2008) p. 202.

Chapter 2: Why We Need Intercultural Competences

1. The development of competency assessment in organizations is described by Jefferey S. Shippmann, Ronald A. Ash, Mariangela Battista et al. (2000) 'The Practice of Competency Modeling', *Personnel Psychology*, 53, pp. 703–40. Popular competences assessed by companies in German-speaking regions are listed in Stefan Höft and Christof Obermann (2010) 'Der Praxiseinsatz von Assessment Centern im deutschsprachigen Raum: Eine zeitliche Verlaufsanalyse basierend auf den Anwenderbefragungen des Arbeitskreises Assessment Center e.V. von 2001 und 2008' (The practical use of assessment centers in German-speaking regions: a time course analysis based on the user surveys of the Arbeitskreis Assessment Center e.V. from 2001 and 2008) *Wirtschaftspsychologie*, 12(2), pp. 5–16.

2. Numerous books and articles on intercultural competence development have been published, especially in the United States and Germany. See, for example, Darla K. Deardorff (ed.) (2009) *The SAGE Handbook of Intercultural Competence* (Thousand Oaks, CA: SAGE); Gundula Gwenn Hiller and Stefanie Vogler-Lipp (eds) (2010) *Schlüsselqualifikation Interkulturelle Kompetenz an Hochschulen. Grundlagen, Konzepte, Methoden* (Key qualification intercultural competence in higher education. Basics, concepts, methods) (Wiesbaden, Germany: Verlag für Sozialwissenschaften); Myron W. Lustig and Jolene Koester (2013) *Intercultural Competence. Interpersonal Communication Across Cultures, 7th edition* (Upper Saddle River, New Jersey: Pearson); Matthias Otten, Alexander Scheitza and Andrea Cnyrim (eds) (2009) *Interkulturelle Kompetenz im Wandel, Volume 1 and 2* (Intercultural competence in transition) (Münster, Germany: LIT Verlag). Google Books Ngram Viewer, an online tool that shows how often words have appeared in books from 1800 onwards, reveals that the use of the term 'intercultural competence' has steadily increased since 1990.

3. See Arjan Verdooren and Maarten Bremer (2012) 'Interculturele Competentie. Bezint eer ge Begint' (Intercultural competence. Look before you leap), in *Opleiding & Ontwikkeling*, Volume 5, pp. 10–14, for a related discussion

of why cross-cultural knowledge alone is insufficient for intercultural effectiveness.

4. In his Developmental Model of Intercultural Sensitivity, Milton J. Bennett proposes six stages of development, of which the first three stages reflect an ethnocentric way of dealing with cultural differences, and the last three stages an ethno-relative approach. People in stage three, which is called minimization, downplay cultural differences and need to focus more on differences in order to develop further. See Milton J. Bennett (1993) 'Towards Ethnorelativism: A Developmental Model of Intercultural Sensitivity', in R. Michael Paige (ed.) *Education for the Intercultural Experience*, 2nd edition (Yarmouth, ME: Intercultural Press).

5. We have not been able to trace the Japanese movie featuring the schoolgirl protesting in public against her teacher. We are grateful to Masako Kato, from Many Truths, for helping us interpret the scene in question.

6. For insightful analyses on French management and business culture, see the landmark analysis by Philippe d'Iribarne (1989) *La Logique de L'Honneur: Gestion des Entreprises et Traditions Nationales* (Paris, France: Édition du Seuil), as well as Jean-Louis Barsoux and Peter A. Lawrence (1997) *French Management: Elitism in Action* (New York, NY: Taylor and Francis); Christoph Barmeyer and Stefanie von Wietersheim (2007) *Business Know-How Frankreich* (Heidelberg: Redline Wirtschaft), and the more recent publication by Philippe d'Iribarne (2012) *Managing Corporate Values in Diverse National Cultures: The Challenge of Differences* (London: Routledge).

7. Christopher Wolsko, Bernadette Park, Charles M. Judd and Bernd Wittenbrink (2000) 'Framing Interethnic Ideology: Effects of Multicultural and Color-blind Perspectives on Judgments of Groups and Individuals', *Journal of Personality and Social Psychology*, Volume 78(4), pp. 635–54.

8. See Wolsko et al. (2000).

9. In one definition of intercultural competence, proposed by Stefanie Rathje, the ability to identify shared group memberships, based on a differentiated view of one's own multiple group memberships, is defined as the core of intercultural competence. See Stefanie Rathje (2007) 'Intercultural Competence', *Journal for Language and Intercultural Communication*, Volume 7(4), pp. 254–66.

10. For a classic study on the psychology of group categorization, see Henri Tajfel (1970) 'Experiments in Intergroup Discrimination', *Scientific American*, Volume 223, pp. 96–102. Numerous studies have shown how categorizing people into groups reduces our ability and willingness to see differences between members of a group. See, for example, Henri Tajfel (ed.) (1982) *Social Identity and Intergroup Relations* (Cambridge, UK: Cambridge University Press); George A. Quattrone and Edward E. Jones (1980)

'The Perception of Variability within In-Groups and Out-Groups: Implications for the Law of Small Numbers', *Journal of Personality and Social Psychology*, Volume 38(1), pp. 141–52; and Charles M. Judd and Bernadette Park (1988) 'Out-Group Homogeneity: Judgments of Variability at the Individual and Group Levels', *Journal of Personality and Social Psychology*, Volume 54(5), pp. 778–88. Overall, members of the out-group are more easily seen as homogeneous, than members of the in-group. A meta-analysis of when and why we perceive in-groups and out-groups as homogeneous has been conducted by Brian Mullen and Li-Tze Hu (1989) 'Perceptions of Ingroup and Outgroup Variability: A Meta-Analytic Integration', *Basic and Applied Social Psychology*, Volume 10(3), pp. 233–52.

11. For the defining experiment on how competition leads to conflict between arbitrarily created groups, see Muzafer Sherif, O. J. Harvey, B. Jack White, William R. Hood and Carolyn W. Sherif (1954/1961) *Intergroup Conflict and Cooperation: The Robbers Cave Experiment* (The University of Oklahoma: Norman).

12. The options for responding to conflict are based on Kenneth W. Thomas and Ralph H. Kilmann (1974) *Thomas-Kilmann Conflict Mode Instrument* (Tuxedo NY: Xicom). For more recent work on conflict behaviour, see Evert van de Vliert (1997) *Complex Interpersonal Conflict Behaviour: Theoretical Frontiers* (Hove, UK: Psychology Press); and Carsten K. W. de Dreu and Evert van de Vliert (eds) (1997) *Using Conflict in Organizations* (Thousand Oaks, CA: SAGE).

13. How the Thomas and Kilmann (1974) conflict management grid can be used for reconciling seemingly opposing cultural values was first shown in the 1993 publication of *Riding the Waves of Culture*, by Fons Trompenaars (London: The Economist). For the revised 3rd edition, see Fons Trompenaars and Charles Hampden-Turner (2011) *Riding the Waves of Culture: Understanding Cultural Diversity in Business* (London: McGraw-Hill).

14. The concept of ego depletion was first proposed by Roy F. Baumeister, T. Heatherton, and Dianne M. Tice in their 1994 publication, *Losing Control: How and Why People Fail at Self-Regulation* (San Diego, CA: Academic Press). For a more recent publication, see Roy F. Baumeister and John Tierney (2011) *Willpower: Rediscovering the Greatest Human Strength* (New York, NY: Penguin Press). An alternative to ego depletion has been proposed by Michael Inzlicht and Brandon J. Schmeichel (2012) 'What is Ego Depletion? Toward a Mechanistic Revision of the Resource Model of Self-Control', *Perspectives on Psychological Science*, Volume 7(5), pp. 450–63.

15. For experiments showing the helpful effects of chocolate on self-control, see Matthew T. Gailliot, Roy F. Baumeister, C. Nathan DeWall, Jon K. Maner, E. Ashby Plant, Dianne M. Tice, Lauren E. Brewer and Brandon J. Schmeichel (2007) 'Self-Control Relies on Glucose as a Limited Energy Source: Willpower

is More Than a Metaphor', *Journal of Personality and Social Psychology*, Volume 92(2), pp. 325–36.

16. Individual differences in how we deal with uncertainty have been analysed by Richard M. Sorrentino and colleagues, and Lily A. Arasaratnam and colleagues. See, for example, Richard M. Sorrentino, Andrew C. H. Szeto, John B. Nezlek, Satoru Yasunaga, Sadafusa Kouhara and Yasunao Otsubo (2008) 'Uncertainty Regulation: The Master Motive?', in Richard M. Sorrentino and Susumu Yamaguchi (eds) *Handbook of Motivation and Cognition Across Cultures* (New York: Elsevier) pp. 49–70; and Lily A. Arasaratnam, Smita C. Banerjee and Krzysztof Dembek (2010) 'Sensation Seeking and the Integrated Model of Intercultural Communication Competence', *Journal of Intercultural Communication Research*, Volume 39(2), pp. 69–79.

Chapter 3: The Four Competences

1. Daniel J. Kealey (1989) 'A Study of Cross-Cultural Effectiveness: Theoretical Issues, Practical Applications', *International Journal of Intercultural Relations*, Volume 13(3), pp. 387–428.

2. Regina Hechanova, Terry A. Beehr, and Neil D. Christiansen (2003) 'Antecedents and Consequences of Employees' Adjustment to Overseas Assignment: A Meta-Analytic review', *Applied Psychology*, Volume 52(2), pp. 213–36.

3. Stefan T. Mol, Marise Ph. Born, M. E. Willemsen and Henk T. van der Molen (2005) 'Predicting Expatriate Job Performance for Selection Purposes: A Quantitative Review', *Journal of Cross-Cultural Psychology*, Volume 36(5), pp. 590–620.

4. Daniel J. Kealey and Brent D. Ruben (1983) 'Cross-Cultural Personnel Selection Criteria, Issues and Methods', in Dan Landis and Richard Brislin (eds) *Handbook of Intercultural Training, Volume 1* (Elmsford, NY: Pergamon) pp. 155–75. Gretchen M. Spreitzer, Morgan McCall Jr, and Joan D. Mahoney (1997) 'Early Identification of International Executive Potential', *Journal of Applied Psychology*, Volume 82(1), pp. 6–29; Joe Jordan and Susan Cartwright (1998) 'Selecting Expatriate Managers: Key Traits and Competencies', *Leadership & Organization Development Journal*, Volume 19(2), pp. 89–96.

5. David C. Thomas and Stacey R. Fitzsimmons (2008) 'Cross-Cultural Skills and Abilities', in Peter B. Smith and Mark F. Peterson (eds) *The Handbook of Cross-Cultural Management Research* (London: SAGE) pp. 201–15.

6. The correlation between scores on Intercultural Sensitivity and management level is r. = 0.06. According to Cohen's guidelines for interpreting effect sizes, this means that there is not even a small effect of management level on

competence scores. See Jacob Cohen (1988) *Statistical Power Analysis for the Behavioral Sciences* (Hillsdale, NJ: Lawrence Erlbaum Associates).

7. The term 'intercultural communication' is defined differently, depending on academic discipline and authors. In anthropology, for example, 'intercultural communication' refers to a method for the appropriate studies of cultures foreign to the researcher. In the behavioural sciences, some authors use it to refer to studies investigating which personality traits and competences, for example, may contribute to successful intercultural communication. But 'intercultural communication' has also been used to refer to the *observable* component of intercultural competence; as an equivalent to 'intercultural competence' and as an equivalent to intercultural effectiveness. In the Intercultural Readiness approach, we use the term 'intercultural communication' to refer to one of four intercultural competences that contribute to intercultural effectiveness. For an overview of different approaches to intercultural communication, see *International Journal of Intercultural Relations, Special Issue: Intercultural Communication Competence*, Volume 13(3), 1989. For a recent discussion, see Thomas and Fitzsimmons (2008).

8. For a discussion on cultural differences in making complaints, see Helen Spencer-Oatey and Peter Franklin (2009) *Intercultural Interaction. A Multidisciplinary Approach to Intercultural Communication* (Basingstoke, UK: Palgrave Macmillan).

9. See Felix C. Brodbeck, Michael Frese, Staffan Akerblom et al. (2000) 'Cultural Variation of Leadership Prototypes Across 22 European Countries', *Journal of Occupational and Organizational Psychology*, Volume 73(1), pp. 1–29; and Jagdeep S. Chhokar, Felix C. Brodbeck and Robert J. House (eds) (2007) *Culture and Leadership Across the World: The GLOBE Book of In-Depth Studies of 25 Societies* (New York: Lawrence Erlbaum Associates).

10. Marianne Schmid Mast, Denise Frauendorfer and Laurence Popovic (2011) 'Self-Promoting and Modest Job Applicants in Different Cultures', *Journal of Personnel Psychology*, Volume 10(2), pp. 70–77.

11. Clarity and effectiveness are two of the five conversational concerns proposed by Min-Sun Kim to explain cultural differences in communication. The other three are 'avoid hurting the hearer's feelings', 'do not impose' and 'avoid being evaluated negatively by the hearer'. See Min-Sun Kim (1994) 'Cross-Cultural Comparisons of the Perceived Importance of Conversational Constraints', *Human Communication Research*, Volume 21(1), pp. 128–51.

12. Penelope Brown and Stephen C. Levinson (1997) *Politeness: Some Universals in Language Usage* (Cambridge, UK: Cambridge University Press).

13. Ute Fischer and Judith Orasanu (2000) 'Error-Challenging Strategies: Their Role in Preventing and Correcting Errors', in *Proceedings of the International Ergonomics Association, 14th Triennial Congress and Human Factors and Ergonomics Society*, 44th Annual Meeting in San Diego, California, August 2000.

14. All examples in this table are derived from Schmid Mast, Frauendorfer and Popovic (2011).

15/16. Schmid Mast, Frauendorfer and Popovic (2011), p. 72.

17. For research on the effects of national cultures on cockpit communication see Robert L. Helmreich (1994) 'Anatomy of a System Accident: The Crash of Avianca Flight 052', *International Journal of Aviation Psychology*, Volume 4(3), pp. 265–84; and Robert L. Helmreich and Ashleigh C. Merritt (2001) *Culture at Work in Aviation and Medicine: National, Organizational, and Professional Influences* (Aldershot: Ashgate).

18. Suggestions for how training can improve crew communication can be found in Ute Fischer and Judith Orasanu (1999) 'Say It Again, Sam! Effective Communication Strategies to Mitigate Pilot Error', in *Proceedings of the 10th International Symposium on Aviation Psychology, Columbus, Ohio, May 1999*; and in Ute Fischer (2000) *Cultural Variability in Crew Discourse*. Final Report on Cooperative Agreement No. NCC 2-933 (http://lmc.gatech. edu/~fischer).

19. For culture-specific analyses of turn-taking in conversation, see, for example, Jaakko Lehtonen and Kari Sajavaara (1985) 'The Silent Finn' (pp. 193–202), and Deborah Tannen (1985) 'Silence: Anything but' (pp. 93–109), both in Deborah Tannen and Muriel Saville-Troike (eds) *Perspectives on Silence* (Norwood, NJ: Ablex).

20. Tanja Stivers, Nick H. Enfield, Penelope Brown et al. (2009) 'Universals and Cultural Variation in Turn-Taking in Conversation', *Proceedings of the National Academy of Sciences of the United States of America*, Volume 106(26), pp. 10587–92.

21. Federico Rossano, Penelope Brown, and Stephen C. Levinson (2009) 'Gaze, Questioning, and Culture', in Jack Sidnell (ed.) *Conversation Analysis: Comparative Perspectives* (Cambridge, UK: Cambridge University Press) pp. 187–249.

22. On gender differences in communication, see Deborah Tannen (1990/2006) *You Just Don't Understand* (New York, NY: HarperCollins).

23. The dilemma reconciliation approach to cultural differences was first proposed by Fons Trompenaars (1993) *Riding the Waves of Culture: Understanding Cultural Diversity in Business* (London: The Economist). For the revised 3rd edition, see Fons Trompenaars and Charles Hampden-Turner (2011) *Riding the Waves of Culture: Understanding Cultural Diversity in Business* (London: McGraw-Hill).

24. The correlation between Building Commitment and management level is r. = 0.201, reflecting a medium-size effect, according to Cohen's guidelines.

25. A recent review of leadership theories is provided by Bruce J. Avolio, Fred O. Walumbwa and Todd J. Weber (2009) 'Leadership: Current Theories, Research, and Future Directions', *Annual Review of Psychology*, Volume 60, pp. 421–49.

26. For studies on transformational leadership, see Bernard M. Bass and Bruce J. Avolio (eds) (1994) *Improving Organizational Effectiveness through Transformational Leadership* (Thousand Oaks, CA: SAGE). For recent work on transformational leadership, see, for example, Bernard M. Brass and Ronald E. Riggio (2012) *Transformational Leadership: Edition 2* (Hove, UK: Psychology Press). The complexity leadership theory has been developed by Mary Uhl-Bien, Russell A. Marion, and Bill McKelvey (2007) 'Complexity Leadership Theory: Shifting Leadership from the Industrial Age to the Knowledge Era', *The Leadership Quarterly*, Volume 18(4), pp. 298–318.

27. Tamara L. Friedrich, William B. Vessey, Matthew J. Schuelke, Gregory A. Ruark and Michael D. Mumford (May 2011) *A Framework for Understanding Collective Leadership: The Selective Utilization of Leader and Team Expertise Within Networks* (United States Army Research Institute for the Behavioral and Social Sciences, Technical Report 1288).

28. Leader-member-exchange theory goes as far back as 1973, when it was proposed by Fred Dansereau, James F. Cashman and George B. Graen. See Dansereau et al. (1973) 'Instrumentality Theory and Equity Theory as Complementary Approaches in Predicting the Relationship of Leadership and Turnover Among Managers', *Organizational Behavior and Human Performance*, Volume 10, pp. 184–200. A meta-analysis of empirical work has been provided by Charlotte R. Gerstner and David V. Day (1997) 'Meta-Analytic Review of Leader-Member Exchange Theory: Correlates and Construct Issues', *Journal of Applied Psychology*, Volume 82, pp. 827–44, and an analysis of the different levels of relationships involved (for example, dyads and teams) can be found in Claudia C. Cogliser and Chester A. Schriesheim (2000) 'Exploring Work Unit Context and Leader-Member Exchange: A Multi-Level Perspective', *Journal of Organizational Behavior*, Volume 21, pp. 487–511.

29. Prasad Balkundi and Martin Kilduff (2006) 'The Ties that Lead: A Social Network Approach to Leadership', *The Leadership Quarterly*, Volume 17, pp. 419–39.

30. The ego network of leaders is described by Balkundi and Kilduff (2006).

31. Jerome Kagan (1971) *Understanding Children: Behavior, Motives, and Thought* (New York: Harcourt Brace Jovanovich). See also the 2002 publication by Jerome Kagan, *Surprise, Uncertainty and Mental Structures* (Cambridge, MA: Harvard University Press).

32. Richard M. Sorrentino, Andrew C. H. Szeto, John B. Nezlek, Satoru Yasunaga, Sadafusa Kouhara, and Yasunao Otsubo (2008) 'Uncertainty Regulation: The Master Motive?', in Richard M. Sorrentino and Susumu Yamaguchi (eds) *Handbook of Motivation and Cognition Across Cultures* (New York, NY: Elsevier) pp. 49–70.

33. Lily A. Arasaratnam and Smita C. Banerjee (2007) 'Ethnocentrism and Sensation Seeking as Variables that Influence Intercultural Contact-Seeking

Behavior: A Path Analysis', *Communication Research Reports*, Volume 24(4), pp. 303–10; and Lily A. Arasaratnam, Smita C. Banerjee and Krzysztof Dembek (2010). 'Sensation Seeking and the Integrated Model of Intercultural Communication Competence', *Journal of Intercultural Communication Research*, Volume 39(2), pp. 69–79.

Chapter 4: Different Talents, New Abilities

1. The farewell scene is on YouTube: available at http://www.youtube.com/watch?v=QJyK2mmjll (accessed 6 Oct 2013). See also Johan Cruyff: At a Given Moment (Johan Cruijff – En un momento dado) by director Ramón Gieling.
2. Jan Pieter van Oudenhoven, Françoise Askevis-Leherpeux, Bettina Hannover, Renske Jaarsma and Benoît Dardenne (2002) 'Asymmetrical international attitudes', *European Journal of Social Psychology*, Volume 32(2), pp. 275–89.

Chapter 5: Intercultural Competences Develop by Themselves: True or False?

1. An excellent discussion on how prior cultural exposure is believed to build the global professional is provided by Paula Caligiuri in her 2012 book, *Cultural Agility. Building a Pipeline of Successful Global Professionals* (San Francisco, CA: Jossey-Bass) pp. 10ff.
2. The need to define more clearly criteria for intercultural effectiveness is argued for by David C. Thomas and Stacey R. Fitzsimmons (2008) 'Cross-Cultural Skills and Abilities', in Peter B. Smith and Mark F. Peterson (eds) *The Handbook of Cross-Cultural Management Research* (London: SAGE) pp. 201–15.
3. Brookfield Global Relocation Services (2012) *Global Relocation Trends: 2012 Survey Report.*
4. That 400-year-old class distinctions still have their effect on today's managerial relationships in France has been convincingly argued by Philippe d'Iribarne (1989) *La Logique de L'Honneur: Gestion des Entreprises et Traditions Nationales* (Paris, France: Édition du Seuil). For empirical studies testing the long-term effects of different cultural traditions in the US, see Richard E. Nisbett and Doy Cohen (1996) *Culture of Honor: The Psychology of Violence in the South* (Colorado: Westview Press).
5. Hilary Harris and Chris Brewster (1999) 'The Coffee-Machine System: How International Selection Really Works', *International Journal of Human*

Resource Management, Volume 10(3), pp. 488–500. The example of the conversation about Simon is based on the description Harris and Brewster provide on p. 497.

6. All data are based on the website of the National Center for O*NET Development: O*NET Resource Center (http://www.onetcenter.org. Retrieved July 13, 2013).

7. See the O*NET Resource Center's summary report 11-9121.02 for information on water resource specialists.

8. The definition of 'knowledge of sociology and anthropology' used by the O*NET can be found on http://www.onetonline.org/find/descriptor/result/2.C.4.f. This page also shows the 30 occupations where this knowledge is most commonly required.

9. Figures are based on:

   – US Census Bureau (May 2012) *The Foreign-Born Population in the United States: 2010* (http://www.census.gov).
   – US Export fact sheet (April 2013) (http://www.trade.gov/press/press-releases/2013/export-factsheet-april2013-040513.pdf).

10. CEDEFOP The European Centre for the Development of Vocational Training, Report No. 30 (2013) *Quantifying Skill Needs in Europe: Occupational Skills Profiles: Methodology and Application* (http://www.cedefop.europa.eu/EN/Files/5530_en.pdf).

11. The CEDEFOP report defines the competence 'general culture/cultural awareness and expression' in line with the definition used by the 'Recommendation of the European Parliament and of the Council of 18 December 2006 on Key Competences for Lifelong Learning', published in the *Official Journal of the European Union*.

12. Figures are based on:

   – Joachim Wagner (2012) 'Neue Fakten über Exporteure und Importeure. Eine Auswertung von Transaktionsdaten für 2009. Wirtschaftsdienst', *Zeitschrift für Wirtschaftspolitik*, Volume 92(7), pp. 496–98.
   – Jean-Christophe Dumont and Georges Lemaître (2008) 'Counting Foreign-Born and Expatriates in OECD Countries: A New Perspective', in James Raymer and Frans Willekens (eds) *International Migration in Europe: Data, Models and Estimates* (Chichester, UK: John Wiley & Sons) pp. 11–40. Centraal Bureau voor de Statistiek (http://www.cbs.nl).

13. European Commission/EACEA/Eurydice (2012) *Developing Key Competences at School in Europe: Challenges and Opportunities for Policy. Eurydice Report* (Luxembourg: Publications Office of the European Union) p. 1.

14. Information on the programme MobiPro-EU can be found on the website of the German Ministerium für Arbeit und Soziales (Ministry for Work and Social Affairs) http://www.bmas.de as well as on www.thejobofmylife.de/en/.
15. The interview with Thomas Liebig was published in *Die ZEIT*, 4 July 2013, p. 63. Translation by the authors.
16. The Language Technology Centre Ltd (2009) *The European Commission's Directorate-General for Translation: The Size of the Language Industry in the EU*.
17. We are grateful to Tom Fadrhonc, ITIM International, for this example of a successful gap year.
18. Information about the history and achievements of the Erasmus programme can be found at http://ec.europa.eu/education/erasmus/history.
19. Intercultural Sensitivity has a significant relationship with age, $F(1, 27284) = 32.613$, $p < .001$, but the size of this effect is $\eta^2 = .005$ and so does not reach the threshold of being a small effect. For the remaining competences, there is a borderline small to small effect of age on increased competence scores: for Building Commitment, it is $F(1, 27284) = 64.172$, $p < .001$, $\eta^2 = .009$; for Intercultural Communication $F(1, 12250) = 26.132$, $p < .001$, $\eta^2 = .008$; and for Managing Uncertainty $F(1, 27284) = 105.898$, $p < .001$, $\eta^2 = .015$.
20. For statistics on the growth of internet and social media usage over this period: International Telecommunication Union (2011) *The World in 2011. ICT Facts and Figures* (Geneva, Switzerland) (http://www.itu.int/ict, retrieved 16 July 2013).
21. For Intercultural Sensitivity, the effect size of the difference between the 2002/03 cohort and the later cohorts is d=0.29; for Managing Uncertainty, it is d=0.27, showing the 2002/03 cohort to have better scores on these two competences than the later cohorts.
22. The information on Europe is based on www.britannica.com.
23. The statistics referring to the United States, The Netherlands and Germany are based on the *CIA World Fact Book* (https://www.cia.gov/library/publications/the-world-factbook).
24. The information about the size of European countries is again based on the *CIA World Fact Book*.
25. The difference in Intercultural Sensitivity scores, with US Americans scoring higher than Europeans, shows a small effect of d=1.22.
26. Edward T. Hall's contribution to the field is captured by E. M. Rogers, W. B. Hart and Y. Miike (2002) 'Edward T Hall and the History of Intercultural Communication: The United States and Japan', *Keio Communication Review*, Volume 24(3), pp. 3–26. How intercultural training developed in the Peace Corps in the 1960s is described by Laurette Bennhold-Samaan (2004) 'The Evolution of Cross-Cultural Training in the Peace Corps', in Dan Landis, Janet M. Bennett and Milton J. Bennett (eds) *Handbook of Intercultural Training*,

3rd edition (Thousand Oaks, CA: SAGE) pp. 363–95. In the same book, see the chapter by Margaret D. Pusch, 'Intercultural Training in Historical Perspective', pp. 13–36.

27. We used the indices developed by Alberto Alesina, Arnaud Devleeschauwer, William Easterly, Sergio Kurlat and Romain Wacziarg (2003) 'Fractionalization', *Journal of Economic Growth*, Volume 8(2), pp. 155–94.

28. See www.standaard.be/cnt/dmf20130721_025 (Retrieved 21 July 2013).

29. The first studies on the 'mere exposure effect' were published by Robert B. Zajonc (1968) 'Attitudinal Effects of Mere Exposure', *Journal of Personality and Social Psychology*, Volume 9(2, Part 2), pp. 1–27. A meta-analysis of findings was published by Robert F. Bornstein and Paul R. d'Agostino (1992) 'Stimulus Recognition and the Mere Exposure Effect', *Journal of Personality and Social Psychology*, Volume 63(4), pp. 545–52.

30. Gordon W. Allport (1954) *The Nature of Prejudice* (Cambridge, MA: Addison-Wesley).

31. Thomas F. Pettigrew and Linda R. Tropp (2011) *When Groups Meet: The Dynamics of Intergroup Contact* (New York, NY: Psychology Press).

32. Marian S. van Bakel (2012) *In Touch with the Dutch. A Longitudinal Study of the Impact of a Local Host on the Success of the Expatriate Assignment* (Centre for PhD Research, Radboud University Nijmegen, The Netherlands).

33. In the report of HSBC Bank International, *The Expat Explorer Survey 2010. Report Two: Expat Experience*, The Netherlands scores lowest on a list of 25 countries when it comes to ease of making friends among the locals.

34. Purnima Bhaskar-Shrinivas, David A. Harrison, Margaret A. Shaffer and Dora M. Luk (2005) 'Input-Based and Time-Based Models of International Adjustment: Meta-Analytic Evidence and Theoretical Extensions', *The Academy of Management Journal,* Volume 48(2), pp. 257–81. In particular, the authors aimed to test, and found support for, an influential model of expatriate adjustment, proposed by Mark E. Mendenhall and Gary Oddou (1985) 'The Dimensions of Expatriate Acculturation: A Review', *The Academy of Management Review*, Volume 10(1), pp. 39–47, and Stewart J. Black, Mark E. Mendenhall and Gary Oddou (1991) 'Toward a Comprehensive Model of International Adjustment: An Integration of Multiple Theoretical Perspectives', *The Academy of Management Review*, Volume 16(2), pp. 291–317.

35. Stefan Mol, Marise Ph. Born, Madde E. Willemsen and Henk van der Molen (2005) 'Predicting Expatriate Job Performance for Selection Purposes: A Quantitative Review', *Journal of Cross-Cultural Psychology*, Volume 36(5), pp. 590–620.

36. We are grateful to Professor Karen van der Zee for suggesting to include questions about respondents' international orientation in our data collection right from the start.

Chapter 6: Intercultural Competences for Culturally Diverse Teams

1. This was the documentary 'Siegen Lernen. Das Geheimnis des Erfolgs' (Learning to win. The secret of success), which was shown on the German TV channel ZDF on 18 June 2010. The experiments involving the chimpanzees were conducted by researchers at the Department of Developmental and Comparative Psychology at the Max Planck Institute for Evolutionary Anthropology in Leipzig, Germany.

2. Alici P. Melis, Anna-Claire Schneider and Michael Tomasello (2011) 'Chimpanzees (Pan Troglodytes) Share Food in the Same Way After Individual and Collaborative Acquisition', *Animal Behaviour*, Volume (82), pp. 485–93.

3. Source: http://www.bpb.de/nachschlagen/zahlen-und-fakten/globalisierung /52630/anzahl (retrieved 15 July 2013).

4. J. Richard Hackman (1998) 'Why Teams Don't Work', in R. Scott Tindale, Linda Heath, John Edwards, Emil J. Posavac, Fred B. Bryant, Judith Myers, Yolanda Suarez-Balcazar and Eaaron Henderson-King (eds) *Theory and Research on Small Groups* (New York, NY: Plenum).

5. See J. Richard Hackman (1998).

6. Katherine Y. Williams and Charles A. O'Reilly (1998) 'Demography and Diversity in Organizations: A Review of 40 years of Research', *Research in Organizational Behavior*, Volume 20, pp. 77–140.

7. Günter Stahl, Martha L. Maznevski, Andreas Voigt and Karsten Jonsen (2010) 'Unraveling the Effects of Cultural Diversity in Teams: A Meta-Analysis of Research on Multicultural Work Groups', *Journal of International Business Studies*, Volume 41, pp. 690–709.

8. For evidence of the negative effects of conflict on teams, see Carsten K. W. de Dreu and Laurie R. Weingart (2003) 'Task and Relationship Conflict, Team Performance, and Team Member Satisfaction: A Meta-Analysis', *Journal of Applied Psychology*, Volume 88, pp. 741–49.

9. Christopher Wolsko, Bernadette Park, Charles M. Judd and Bernd Wittenbrink (2000) 'Framing Interethnic Ideology: Effects of Multicultural and Color-blind Perspectives on Judgments of Groups and Individuals', *Journal of Personality and Social Psychology*, Volume 78(4), pp. 635–54.

10. See Stahl et al. (2010).

11. Tina Girndt (2000) *Cultural Diversity and Work-Group Performance: Detecting the Rules* (Tilburg, NL: CentER, Tilburg University).

12. For a recent review of research on team diversity and performance, as well as references to relevant literature, see Daan van Knippenberg and Michaéla C. Schippers (2007) 'Work Group Diversity', *Annual Review of Psychology*, Volume 58, pp. 515–41.

13. See Williams and O'Reilly (1998) and Knippenberg and Schippers (2007) for reviews of studies investigating effects of different diversity criteria.

14. Evidence that 'other than job-related' criteria of diversity contribute to performance has recently been provided by Hans van Dijk, Marloes L. van Engen and Daan van Knippenberg (2012) 'Defying Conventional Wisdom: A Meta-Analytical Examination of the Differences Between Demographic and Job-Related Diversity Relationships with Performance', *Organizational Behavior and Human Decision Processes*, Volume 119, pp. 38–53.

15. See Patricia O'Toole (1989) 'Battle of the Beauty Counter', *The New York Times*, 3 December 1989. Retrieved from http://www.nytimes.com/1989/12/03/maga-zine/battle-of-the-beauty-counter.html?pagewanted=all&src=pm on 15 July 2013.

16. The two processes affecting diverse teams are typically discussed in terms of the Social Categorization perspective, on the one hand, and the Infor-mation/Decision-making perspective, on the other hand. An integration of both perspectives into an interactive causal model has been proposed by Daan van Knippenberg, Carsten K. W. de Dreu and Astrid C. Homan in their categorization-elaboration model. See van Knippenberg et al. (2004) 'Work Group Diversity and Group Performance: An Integrative Model and Research Agenda', *Journal of Applied Psychology*, Volume 89, pp. 1008–22.

17. See, for example, Henri Tajfel and John C. Turner (1986) 'The Social Identity Theory of Intergroup Behavior', in S. Worchel and W. Austin (eds) *Psychol-ogy of Intergroup Relations* (Chicago: Nelson-Hall) pp. 7–24; and John C. Turner, Michael A. Hogg, Penelope J. Oakes, Stephen D. Reicher and Margaret S. Wetherell (1987) *Rediscovering the Social Group: A Self-Categorization Theory* (Oxford, UK: Blackwell).

18. For analyses of group discussions, a new instrument has been developed by Carsten C. Schermuly and Wolfgang Scholl (2012) 'The Discussion Coding System (DCS): A New Instrument for Analyzing Communication Processes', *Communication Methods and Measures*, Volume 6, pp. 12–40. See also the book publication in German by Schermuly and Scholl (2011) *Instrument zur Kodierung von Diskussionen (IKD)* (Göttingen, Germany: Hogrefe).

19. The concept of faultlines as a key to understanding diversity and team performance was first proposed by Dora C. Lau and I. Keith Murnighan (1998) 'Demographic Diversity and Faultlines: The Compositional Dynamics of Organizational Groups', *Academy of Management Review*, Volume 23, pp. 325–40. It has inspired numerous studies investigating the role of fault-lines to explain the negative effects of diversity on team performance.

20. See Lau and Murnighan (1998)

21. See the work by van Knippenberg et al. (2004) on the categorization-elaboration model.

22. The story of how Art Fry realized the potential of Spencer Silver's weak adhesive glue is told on several websites and articles on the internet. For the story and quote below, see http://www.post-it.com/wps/portal/3M/en_US/Post_It/Global/About (retrieved 15 July 2013).

23. The Bay of Pigs decision and the failure to foresee the attack on Pearl Harbor were first explained as a result of groupthink by Irving L. Janis (1972/1982) *Victims of Groupthink: A Psychological Study of Foreign-Policy Decisions and Fiascoes* (Boston: Houghton Mifflin). Explaining the Swissair collapse in terms of groupthink was proposed by Aaron Hermann and Hussain G. Rammal (2010) 'The Grounding of the "Flying Bank"', *Management Decision*, Volume 48(7), pp. 1048–62.

24. How diversity affects teams over time has in particular been investigated by D. A. Harrison and his team. See, for example, D. A. Harrison, K. H. Price, J. H. Gavin and A. T. Florey (2002) 'Time, Teams, and Task Performance: Changing Effects of Surface- and Deep-Level Diversity on Group Functioning', *Academy of Management Journal*, Volume 45, pp. 1029–45. Van Knippenberg and Schippers (2007) propose that in highly diverse organizations, diversity in teams will be easier for team members to deal with than in less diverse organizations, because the team's diversity does not stick out as something special. In their landmark study on diversity perspectives, Robin J. Ely and David A. Thomas show that only a perspective on diversity as a source for learning, integration and change is feasible in the long run. See Ely and Thomas (2001) 'Cultural Diversity at Work: The Effects of Diversity Perspectives on Work Group Processes and Outcomes', *Administrative Science Quarterly*, Volume 46(2), pp. 229–73.

25. Michael Lewis (2003) *Moneyball. The Art of Winning an Unfair Game* (New York, London: WW Norton & Company).

26. In *Moneyball* (2003), page 18, you will find a wonderful description of Paul DePodesta's affinity with irrationality.

27. And go to *Moneyball* (2003), pages 16–17, for an even more graphic description of the scene.

28. All information on player salaries and baseball games are taken from Wikipedia.org (retrieved 15 July 2013).

29. Daan van Knippenberg, S. Alexander Haslam and Michael J. Platow (2007) *Unity through Diversity: Value-in-Diversity Beliefs, Work Group Diversity, and Group Identification*, ERIM report series Research in Management.

30. Sebastian Stegmann (2011) 'Engaging with Diversity of Social Units. A Social Identity Perspective on Diversity in Organizations', PhD thesis, Johann Wolfgang Goethe-Universität Frankfurt am Main, Germany.

31. Francis J. Flynn (2005) 'Having an Open Mind: The Impact of Openness to Experience on Interracial Attitudes and Impression Formation', *Journal of Personality and Social Psychology*, Volume 88(5), pp. 816–26.

32. Astrid C. Homan, Daan van Knippenberg, Gerben van Kleef and Carsten K. W. de Dreu (2007) 'Bridging Faultlines by Valuing Diversity: Diversity Beliefs, Information Elaboration, and Performance in Diverse Work Groups', *Journal of Applied Psychology*, Volume 92(5), pp. 1189–99.

33. Karen I. van Oudenhoven-van der Zee, Paul Paulus, Menno Vos and Niveditha Parthasarathy (2009) 'The Impact of Group Composition and Attitudes Towards Diversity on Anticipated Outcomes of Diversity in Groups', *Group Processes & Intergroup Relations*, Volume 12, pp. 257–80.

34. See again van Knippenberg et al. (2007).

35. Astrid C. Homan, Lindred L. Greer, Karen A. Jehn and Lukas Koning (2010) 'Believing Shapes Seeing: The Impact of Diversity Beliefs on the Construal of Group Composition', *Group Processes & Intergroup Relations*, Volume 13, pp. 477–93.

36. See Homan et al. (2010), page 480, for information on both scales.

37. The correlations between IRC competences and people's diversity beliefs range from 0.260 for Intercultural Communication and 0.269 for Intercultural Sensitivity, to 0.320 for Managing Uncertainty and even up to 0.368 for Building Commitment. That is, the strength of *all* correlations of the IRC competences with diversity beliefs is well above what is considered a small effect (when a correlation of around 0.1 is found). For Building Commitment and Managing Uncertainty, the effect is even well above what is considered a medium-sized effect (correlations around 0.3).

38. Astrid C. Homan and Lindred L. Greer (2013) 'Considering Diversity: The Positive Effects of Considerate Leadership in Diverse Teams', *Group Processes & Intergroup Relations*, Volume 16, pp. 105–25.

39. Lynda Gratton, Andreas Voigt and Tamara J. Erickson (2007) 'Bridging Faultlines in Diverse Teams', *MIT Sloan Management Review*, Volume 48(4), pp. 22–9.

40. The correlation between Managing Uncertainty and subgroup perception was 0.145, a highly significant correlation with a noteworthy effect size.

Chapter 7: What Makes an Organization Interculturally Competent?

1. Annemarie C. J. Kohne (2007) 'Een Onderzoek naar Verschillen in Interculturele Vaardigheden bij Verschillende Bedrijfstakken' (A study on the differences in intercultural competences in different industries), Master thesis at the Department of Psychology, University of Amsterdam, The Netherlands.

2. We classified companies into industries and sectors based on the North American Industry Classification System (NAICS). The NAICS works with 20 main sectors,

each of which is broken down into up to six levels of subsectors. The NAICS is freely accessible online via http://www.census.gov/eos/www/naic/.

3. R. Roosevelt Thomas Jr (1990) 'From Affirmative Action to Affirming Diversity' *Harvard Business Review*, March–April 1990, pp. 107–17.

4. Anneke M. Sools, Marloes L. van Engen and Chris Baerveldt (2007) 'Gendered Career-Making Practices: On "Doing Ambition" or How Managers Discursively Position Themselves in a Multinational Corporation', *Journal of Occupational and Organizational Psychology*, Volume 80, pp. 413–35.

5. Robin J. Ely and David A. Thomas (2001) 'Cultural Diversity at Work: The Moderating Effects of Work Group Perspectives on Diversity', *Administrative Science Quarterly*, Volume 46, pp. 229–73.

6. See Ely and Thomas (2001), pp. 234ff.

Index

Printed and bound by CPI Group (UK) Ltd, Croydon, CR0 4YY